**The Black Man: His Antecede**

By
William W. Brown

# PREFACE.

THE calumniators and traducers of the Negro are to be found, mainly, among two classes. The first and most relentless are those who have done them the greatest injury, by being instrumental in their enslavement and consequent degradation. They delight to descant upon the "natural inferiority" of the blacks, and claim that we were destined only for a servile condition, entitled neither to liberty nor the legitimate pursuit of happiness. The second class are those who are ignorant of the characteristics of the race, and are the mere echoes of the first. To meet and refute these misrepresentations, and to supply a deficiency, long felt in the community, of a work containing sketches of individuals who, by their own genius, capacity, and intellectual development, have surmounted the many obstacles which slavery and prejudice have thrown in their way, and raised themselves to positions of honor and influence, this volume was written. The characters represented in most of these biographies are for the first time put in print. The author's long sojourn in Europe, his opportunity of research amid the archives of England and France, and his visit to the West Indies, have given him the advantage of information respecting the blacks seldom acquired.

If this work shall aid in vindicating the Negro's character, and show that he is endowed with those intellectual and amiable qualities which adorn and dignify human nature, it will meet the most sanguine hopes of the writer.

CAMBRIDGEPORT, MASS., 1863.

# MEMOIR OF THE AUTHOR.

I WAS born at Lexington, Kentucky. My father, as I was informed, was a member of the Wickliffe family; my mother was of mixed blood; her father, it was said, was the noted Daniel Boone, and her mother a negress. My early life on the plantation was such as generally falls to the lot of the young slave, till I arrived at the age of nine years, when my position was changed. My master's brother lost his wife, she leaving an infant son a few months old, whom my mistress took to bring up. When this boy became old enough to need a playmate to watch over him, mistress called the young slaves together, to select one for the purpose. We were all ordered to run, jump, wrestle, turn somersets, walk on our hands, and go through the various gymnastic exercises that the imagination of our brain could invent, or the strength and activity of our limbs could endure. The selection was to be an important one, both to the mistress and the slave. Whoever should gain the place was in the future to become a house servant; the ask-cake thrown aside, that unmentionable garment that buttons around the neck, which we all wore, and nothing else, was to give way to the whole suit of tow linen. Every one of us joined heartily in the contest, while old mistress sat on the piazza, watching our every movement--some fifteen of us, each dressed in his one garment, sometimes standing on our heads with feet in the air--still the lady looked on. With me it seemed a matter of life and death; for, being blood kin to master, I felt that I had more at stake than my companions. At last the choice was made, and I was told to step aside as the "lucky boy," which order I obeyed with an alacrity seldom surpassed. That night I was put to soak, after which I was scraped, scrubbed, washed, and dried. The next day, the new suit came down to the quarters; I slipped into it; the young slaves gathered about me, and I was the star of the plantation. My mother, one of the best of mothers, placed her hands on my head, and, with tears in her eyes, said, "I knowed you was born for good luck, for a fortune-teller told me so when you was a baby layin' in your little sugar trough. Go up to de great house where you belong." With this blessing I bade farewell to the log hut and the dirt floor, and started towards the "big house." Mistress received me, and laid down the law which was to govern my future actions. "I give your young master over to you," said she; "and if you let him hurt himself, I'll pull your ears; if you let him cry, I'll pull your ears; if he wants any thing, and you don't give it to him, I'll pull your ears; when he goes to sleep, if you let him wake before it is time, I'll pull your ears." And right well did she keep her promise, for my ears felt the impress of her tender fingers and gold rings almost every day, and at times nearly every hour.

Yet I would not have you suppose, gentle reader, that my old mistress was of low or common origin; but on the contrary, she boasted that the best blood of the south coursed through her blue veins. My master, Dr. John Young, was a man of considerable standing in his section of the state. A member of the church, his set was not often empty during religious service. He was very strict as to the observance of the Sabbath, held prayer night and morning, and entertained more travelling preachers than almost any one in his neighborhood.

The doctor did not surpass his wife in devotedness to religious observances. Of these travelling ministers, each had a favorite, who in turn used to spend several days on the plantation, hunting, shooting, fishing, visiting, and at times preaching. The Rev. Mr. Pinchen was my mistress's favorite, and he was indeed an interesting character. Short and stout, somewhat inclined to corpulency, deeply pock-marked, quick in his motions, and with a strong voice, he was one of the funniest of men when telling his long stories about his religious and other experiences in the south.

I had been in the great house nearly three years, when Mr. Pinchen was expected to make his annual visit. The stir about the dwellings, the cleaning of paint, the scalding out of the bedbugs, an the orders and counter-orders from Mrs. Young, showed plainly that something uncommon was to take place. High and angry words had passed between master and mistress, one morning, when the latter weepingly and snuffingly exclaimed, "Never mind; you'll not have me here always to hector and to worry: I'll die one of these days, and then you'll be glad of it. Never mind, keep on, and you'll send me to my grave before the time. Never mind; one of these days the Lord will make up his jewels, call me home to glory, and I'll be out of your way, and I'll be devilish glad of it too." Her weeping increased, and she continued, "Never mind, brother Pinchen will be here soon, and then I'll have somebody to talk to me about religion." At this moment, Hannah, the waiting maid, entered the room, and Mrs. Young gave orders with regard to Mr. Pinchen's visit. "Go, Hannah," said she, "and get the chamber ready for brother Pinchen: put on the new linen sheets, and see that they are dry, and well aired; if they are not, I'll air you, my lady." The arrival of the clergyman, the next day, was the signal for new and interesting scenes. After the first morning's breakfast was over, family prayer finished, the Bible put away, the brandy replaced in the sideboard, and Dr. Young gone to his office, Mr. Pinchen commenced the delivery of one of those religious experiences for which be was so celebrated wherever he was known. Mrs. Young and the minister were seated at the round table, I standing behind her chair, and Hannah clearing off the breakfast table, when the servant of God began by saying, "Well, sister Young, I've seen a heap since I was here last."

"I am so glad to hear it," responded she, "for I want to bear something good. Now do give me your experience, brother Pinchen; it always draws me nearer and nearer to the Lord's side."

"Well, sister Young, I've had great opportunity in my time to study the human heart. I've attended a great many camp meetings, revival meetings, protracted meetings, and death-bed scenes, and I am satisfied, sister Young, that the heart of man is full of sin and desperately wicked. This is a wicked world, sister, a wicked world."

Mrs. Young asked, "Were you ever in Arkansas, brother Pinchen? I've been told that the people out there are very ungodly."

Mr. Pinchen said, "O, yes, sister Young; I once spent a year at Little Rock, and preached in all the towns round about there; and I found some hard cases out there, I can tell you. I was once spending a week in a district where there were a great many horse thieves, and one night somebody stole my pony. Well, I knowed it was no use to make a fuss; so I told brother Tarbox to say nothing about it, and I'd get my horse by preaching God's everlasting gospel; for I had faith in the truth, and knowed that my Saviour would not let me lose my pony. So the next Sunday I preached on horse-stealing, and told the brethren to come up in the evenin' with their hearts filled with the grace of God. So that night the house was crammed brim full with anxious souls, panting for the bread of life. Brother Bingham opened with prayer, and brother Tarbox followed, and I saw right off that we were gwine to have a blessed time. After I got 'em pretty well warmed up, I jumped on to one of the seats, stretched out my hands, and said: 'I know who stole my pony; I've found out; and you are here tryin' to make people believe that you've got religion; but you ain't got it. And if you don't take my horse back to brother Tarbox's pasture this very night, I'll tell your name right out in meetin' to-mor-row night. Take my pony back, you vile and wretched sinner, and come up here and give your heart to God.' So the next mornin', I went out to brother Tarbox's pasture, and sure enough, there was my bob-tail pony. Yes, sister, there he was, safe and sound. Ha, ha, ha!"

With uplifted hands, old mistress exclaimed, "O, how interesting, and how fortunate for you to get your pony! And what power there is in the gospel! God's children are very lucky. O, it is so sweet to sit here and listen to such good news from God's people!"

Hannah was so entranced with the conversation that she had left her work, and, with eyes and mouth open, was listening to the preacher. Turning aside, and in a low voice, Mrs. Young harshly said, "Hannah, what are you standing there listening for, and neglecting your work? Never mind, my lady, I'll whip you well when I am done here. Go at your work this moment, you lazy hussy. Never mind, I'll whip you well." Then, turning again to the preacher, she said, "Come, do go on, brother Pinchen, with your godly conversation. It is so sweet! It draws me nearer and nearer to the Lord's side."

"Well, sister Young," continued he, "I've had some mighty queer dreams in my time--that I have. You see, one night I dreamed that I was dead and in heaven; and such a place I never saw before. As soon as I entered the gates of the celestial empire, I saw many old and familiar faces that I had seen before. The first person that I saw was good old Elder Pike, the preacher that first called my attention to religion. The next person I saw was Deacon Billings, my first wife's father; and then I saw a host of godly faces. Why, sister Young, you knew Elder Goosbee--didn't you?"

"Yes," replied she; "did you see him there?"

"O yes, sister Young, I saw the elder, and he looked for all the world as if he had just come out of a revival meeting."

"Did you see my first husband there, brother Pinchen?"

"No, sister Young, I didn't see brother Pepper, but I've no doubt but that he was there."

"Well, I don't know," said she; "I have my doubts. He was not the happiest man in the world. He was always borrowing trouble about something or another. Still, I saw some happy moments with Mr. Pepper. I was happy when I made his acquaintance, happy during our courtship, happy a while after our marriage, and happy when he died."

Here she put her handkerchief to her eyes, and wept bitterly for a moment. At this juncture Hannah asked, "Did you see my husband, Ben, up in hebben, Massa Pinchen?"

"No, no, Hannah, I didn't go amongst the blacks," answered he.

"Of course not," said mistress; "brother Pinchen didn't go among the niggers." Turning aside to Hannah, and in a whisper, she exclaimed, "What are you asking questions for? Never mind, my lady, I'll whip you well when I'm done here. I'll skin you from head to foot. Do go on with your heavenly conversation, brother Pinchen; it does my very soul good. This is indeed a precious moment for me. I do love to hear of Christ and him crucified."

After the conversation had ceased, and the preacher gone out to call on Mrs. Daniels, Mrs. Young said to the maid, "Now, Hannah, brother Pinchen is gone; you get the cowhide, and I'll whip you well, for aggravating me as you did to-day. It seems as if I can never sit down to take a little comfort with the Lord, without the devil putting it into your head to cross me. I've no doubt, Hannah,that I'll miss going to heaven on your account; but I'll whip you well before I leave this world--that I will." The servant received a flogging, Mrs. Young felt easier, and I was in the kitchen amusing my fellow-slaves. with telling over Mr. Pinchen's last experience. Here let me say, that we regarded the religious profession of the whites around us as a farce, and our master and mistress, together with their guest, as mere hypocrites. During the entire visit of the preacher, the servants had a joyful time over my representations of what was going on in the great house.

The removal of my master's family and slaves to the centre of the State of Missouri about this time, caused some change in our condition. My young master, William, had now grown to be a stout boy of five years of age. No restraint thrown around him by the doctor or his wife, aunt Dolly, his nurse, not permitted to control any of his actions, William had become impudent, petulant, peevish and cruel. Sitting at the tea table, he would often desire to make his entire meal out of the sweetmeats, the sugar-bowl, or the cake; and when mistress would not allow him to have them, he, in a fit of anger, would throw any thing within his reach at me; spoons, knives, forks, and dishes would be hurled at my head, accompanied with language such as would astonish any one not well versed in the injurious effects of slavery upon the rising generation. Thomas Jefferson, in 1788, in a letter to M. Warville, Paris, writing upon slavery, alludes to its influence upon the young as follows:--

"The parent storms, the child looks on, catches the lineaments of wrath, puts on the same airs in the circle of smaller slaves, GIVES LOOSE TO HIS WORST PASSIONS; and, thus nursed, educated, and daily exercised in tyranny, cannot but be stamped by it with odious peculiarities."

In the Virginia legislature, in the year 1832, Hon. Lewis Summers said,--

"A slave population exercises the most pernicious influence upon the manners, habits and character of those whom it exists. Lisping infancy learns the vocabulary of abusive epithets, and struts, the embryo tyrant of its little domain. The consciousness of superior destiny takes possession of his mind at its earliest dawning, and love of power and rule 'grows with his growth and strengthens with his strength.' Unless enabled to rise above the operation of those powerful causes, he enters the world with miserable notions of self-importance, and under the government of an unbridled temper."

Having, by speculation and mismanagement, lost the most of his property, Dr. Young resumed the practice of medicine in Missouri, and soon obtained a lucrative run of custom. Here, as in Kentucky, the doctor took great interest in matters of religion, and was considered one of the pillars in the church.

Being sent one Sabbath morning to carry the sacramental wine to the church, about a mile distant, I could not withstand the temptation it presented of tasting it. Having had one swallow, I was tempted further on, till the beverage disappeared out of the neck of the bottle, so that I felt afraid that if noticed by master, I should be flogged. It occurred to me that I might fill up the bottle from one of the sap tubs, as I passed through the sugar camp; for it was the spring of the year, and we were making maple sugar. I tried to pour the sap into the bottle, but it flared over the top, leaving the wine still some inches down the neck. After ransacking my inventive faculties, I fortunately bit upon a plan and filled it up. Placing the bottle on the ground, and sucking my mouth full of the juice, I stood directly over the bottle and let it stream in until it was full. Putting the stopple in, I started off towards the church, feeling that I had got the advantage of master once more.

My fair complexion was a great obstacle to my happiness,both with whites and blacks, in and about the great house. Often mistaken by strangers for a white boy, it annoyed my mistress very much. On one occasion, a visitor came to the place in the absence of the doctor. While Mrs. Young was entertaining the major (for he was a military man), I passed through the room, and going near the stranger, he put out his hand and said to me, "How do you do, bub?" and turning to the lady, he exclaimed, "Madam, I would have known that he was the doctor's son, if I had met him in California, for he is so much like his papa." Mistress ordered me out of the room, and remarked that I was one of the servants, when the major begged pardon for the mistake. After the stranger was gone, I was flogged for his blunder.

Dr. Young sold his large farm, which was situated in the central part of the state, and removed to St. Louis, where a number of the servants were let out. I was put to work tending upon the hands in the office of the "St. Louis Times," a newspaper owned and published by Lovejoy & Miller, and edited by Elijah P. Lovejoy. Here my young heart began to feel more longings for liberty. The love of freedom is a sentiment natural to the human heart, and the want of it is felt by him who does not possess it. He feels it a reproach; and with this sting, this wounded pride, hating degradation, and looking forward to the cravings of the heart, the enslaved is always on the alert for an opportunity to escape from his oppressors and to avenge his wrongs. What greater injury and indignity can be offered to man, than to make him the bond-slave of his fellow-man?

My sojourn in the printing office was of short duration, and I was afterwards let out to a slave-trader named Walker. This heartless, cruel, ungodly man, who neither loved his Maker nor feared Satan, was a fair representative of thousands of demons in human form that are engaged in buying and selling God's children.

One year with Walker, beholding scenes of cruelty that can be better imagined than described, I was once more taken home, and soon after hired out as an under steward on the steamer Patriot, running to New Orleans. This opened to me a new life, and gave me an opportunity to see different phases of slave life, and to learn something more of the world. Life on the Mississippi River is an exciting one. I had not been on the boat but a few weeks when one of those races for which the southern steamers are so famous took place.

At eight o'clock on the evening of the third day of the passage, the lights of another steamer were seen in the distance, and apparently coming up very fast. This was the signal for a general commotion on board the Patriot, and every thing indicated that a steamboat race was at hand. Nothing can exceed the excitement attendant upon the racing of steamers on the Mississippi.

By the time the boats had reached Memphis they were side by side, and each exerting itself to get in advance of the other. The night was clear, the moon shining brightly, and the boats so near to each other that the passengers were within speaking distance. On board the Patriot the firemen were using oil, lard, butter, and even bacon, with wood, for the purpose of raising the steam to its highest pitch. The blaze mingled with the black smoke that issued from the pipes of the other boat, which showed that she also was burning something more combustible than wood.

The firemen of both boats, who were slaves, were singing songs such as can only be heard on board a southern steamer. The boats now came abreast of each other, and nearer and nearer, until they were locked so that men could pass from one to the other. The wildest excitement prevailed among the men employed on the steamers, in which the passengers freely participated.

At this moment the engineer of the Patriot was seen to fasten down the safety-valve, so that no steam should escape. This was indeed a dangerous resort, and a few who saw what had taken place, fearing that an explosion would be the consequence, left that part of the boat for more secure quarters.

The Patriot now stopped to take in passengers; but still no steam was permitted to escape. On the starting of the boat again, cold water was forced into the boilers by the feed-pumps, and, as might have been expected, one of the boilers exploded with terrific force, carrying away the boiler deck and tearing to pieces much of the machinery. One dense fog of steam filled every part of the vessel, while shrieks, groans, and cries were heard on every side. Men were running hither and thither looking for their wives, and women were flying about, in the wildest confusion, seeking for their husbands. Dismay appeared on every countenance.

The saloons and cabins soon looked more like hospitals than any thing else; but by this time the Patriot had drifted to the shore, and the other steamer had come alongside to render assistance to the disabled boat. The killed and wounded (nineteen in number) were put on shore, and the Patriot, taken in tow by the Washington, was once more on her journey.

It was half past twelve, and the passengers, instead of retiring to their berths, once more assembled at the gaming tables. The practice of gambling on the western waters has long been a source of annoyance to the more moral persons who travel on our great rivers. Thousands of dollars often change owners during a passage from St. Louis or Louisville to New Orleans on a Mississippi steamer. Many men are completely ruined on such occasions, and duels are often the consequence.

"Go call my boy, steward," said Mr. Jones, as he took his cards one by one from the table.

In a few minutes a fine-looking, bright-eyed mulatto boy, apparently about sixteen years of age, was standing by his master's side at the table.

"I am broke, all but my boy," said Jones, as he ran his fingers through his cards; "but he is worth a thousand dollars, and I will bet the half of him."

"I will call you," said Thompson, as he laid five hundred dollars at the feet of the boy, who was standing on the table, and at the same time throwing down his cards before his adversary.

"You have beaten me," said Jones; and a roar of laughter followed from the other gentleman as poor Joe stepped down from the table.

"Well, I suppose I owe you half the nigger," said Thompson, as he took hold of Joe and began examining his limbs.

"Yes," replied Jones, "he is half yours. Let me have five hundred dollars, and I will give you a bill of sale of the boy."

"Go back to your bed," said Thompson to his chattel, "and remember that you now belong to me."

The poor slave wiped the tears from his eyes, as, in obedience, he turned to leave the table.

"My father gave me that boy," said Jones, as he took the money, "and I hope, Mr.

Thompson, that you will allow me to redeem him."

"Most certainly, sir," replied Thompson; "whenever you hand over the cool thousand the negro is yours."

Next morning, as the passengers were assembling in the cabin and on deck, and while the slaves were running about waiting on or looking for their masters, poor Joe was seen entering his new master's state-room, boots in hand.

Such is the uncertainty of a slave's life. He goes to bed at night the pampered servant of his young master, with whom he has played in childhood, and who would not see his slave abused under any consideration, and gets up in the morning the property of a man whom he has never before seen.

To behold five or six tables in the saloon of a steamer, with half a dozen men playing cards at each, with money, pistols, and bowie-knives spread in splendid confusion before them, is an ordinary thing on the Mississippi River.

Continued intercourse with educated persons, and meeting on the steamer so many travellers from the free states, caused me to feel more keenly my degraded and unnatural situation. I gained much information respecting the north and Canada that was valuable to me, and I resolved to escape with my mother, who had been sold to a gentleman in St. Louis. The attempt was made, but we were unsuccessful. I was then sold to Mr. Samuel Willi, a merchant tailor. I was again let out to be employed on a Mississippi steamboat, but was soon after sold to Captain E. Price, of the Chester. To escape from slavery and become my own master, was now the ruling passion of my life. I would dream at night that I was free, and, on awaking, weep to find myself still a slave.

"I would think of Victoria's domain;
In a moment I seemed to be there;
But the fear of being taken again
Soon hurried me back to despair."

Thoughts of the future, and my heart yearning for liberty, kept me always planning to escape.

The long-looked-for opportunity came, and I embraced it. Leaving the steamer upon which my now master had me at work, I started for the north, travelling at night and lying by during the day. It was in the winter season, and I suffered much from cold and hunger. Supposing every person to be my enemy, I was afraid to appeal to any one, even for a little food, to keep body and soul together. As I pressed forward, my escape to Canada seemed certain, and this feeling gave me a light heart; for

"Behind I left the whips and chains,
Before me were sweet Freedom's plains."

While on my journey at night, and passing farms, I would seek a corn-crib, and supply myself with some of its contents. The next day, while buried in the forest, I would make a fire and roast my corn, and drink from the nearest stream. One night, while in search of corn, I came upon what I supposed to be a hill of potatoes, buried in the ground for want of a cellar. I obtained a sharp-pointed piece of wood, with which I dug away for more than an hour, and on gaining the hidden treasure, found it to be turnips. However, I did not dig for nothing. After supplying myself with about half a dozen of the turnips, I again resumed my journey. This uncooked food was indeed a great luxury, and gave strength to my fatigued limbs. The weather was very cold,--so cold, that it drove me one night into a barn, where I lay in the hay until morning. A storm overtook me when about a week out. The rain fell in torrents, and froze as it came down. My clothes became stiff with ice. Here again I took shelter in a barn, and walked about to keep from freezing. Nothing but the fear of being arrested and returned to slavery prevented me, at this time, seeking shelter in some dwelling.

After many days of weary travelling, and sick from ex- exposure, I determined to seek shelter and aid; and for this purpose, I placed myself behind some fallen trees near the main road, hoping to see some colored person, thinking I should be more safe under the care of one of my own color. Several farmers with their teams passed, but the appearance of each one frightened me out of the idea of asking for assistance. After lying on the ground for some time, with my sore, frost-bitten feet benumbed with cold, I saw an old, white-haired man, dressed in a suit of drab, with a broad-brimmed bat, walking along, leading a horse. The man was evidently walking for exercise. I came out from my hiding-place and told the stranger I must die unless I obtained some assistance. A moment's conversation satisfied the old man that I was one of the oppressed, fleeing from the house of bondage. From the difficulty with which I walked, the shivering of my limbs, and the trembling of my voice, he became convinced that I had been among thieves, and be acted the part of the Good Samaritan. This was the first person I had ever seen of the religious sect called "Quakers," and his name was Wells Brown. I remained here about a fortnight, and being fitted out with clothes, shoes, and a little money, by these good people, I was again ready to resume my journey. I entered their house with the single name that I was known by at the south, "William;" I left it with the one I now bear.

A few days more, and I arrived at Cleveland, Ohio, where I found employment during the remainder of the winter. Having no education, my first thoughts went in that direction. Obtaining a situation the following spring on a Lake Erie Steamer, I found that I could be very serviceable to slaves who were escaping from the south to Canada. In one year alone I assisted sixty fugitives in crossing to the British queen's dominions. Many of these escapes were attended with much interest. On one occasion, a fugitive had been hid away in the house of a noted abolitionist in Cleveland for ten days, while his master was in town, and watching every steamboat and vessel that left the port. Several officers were also on the watch, guarding the house of the abolitionist every night. The slave was a young and valuable man, of twenty-two years of age, and very black. The friends of the slave had almost despaired of getting him away from his hiding-place, when I was called in, and consulted as to the best course to be taken. I at once inquired if a painter could be found who would paint the fugitive white. In an hour, by my directions, the black man was as white, and with as rosy cheeks, as any of the Anglo-Saxon race, and disguised in the dress of a woman, with a thick veil over her face. As the steamer's bell was tolling for the passengers to come on board, a tall lady, dressed in deep mourning, and leaning on the arm of a gentleman of more than ordinary height, was seen entering the ladies' cabin of the steamer North America, who took her place with the other ladies. Soon the steamer left the wharf, and the slave-catcher and his officers, who had been watching the boat since her arrival, went away, satisfied that their slave had not escaped by the North America, and returned to guard the house of the abolitionist. After the boat had got out of port, and fairly on her way to Buffalo, I showed the tall lady to her state-room. The next morning, the fugitive, dressed in his plantation suit, bade farewell to his native land, crossed the Niagara River, and took up his abode in Canada.

I remained on Lake Erie during the sailing season, and resided in Buffalo in the winter. In the autumn of 1843 I was invited by the officers of the Western New York Anti-Slavery Society to take an agency as a lecturer in behalf of my enslaved countrymen, which offer I accepted, and soon commenced my labors. Mobs were very frequent in those days. Being advertised to address the citizens of Aurora, Erie County, New York, on one occasion, I went to fulfil the appointment, and found the church surrounded by a howling set of men and boys, waiting to give me a warm reception. I went in, opened the meeting, and began my address. But they were resolved on having a good time, and the disturbance was so great that I had to stop. In the mean time, a bag of flour had been brought to the church, taken up into the belfry, directly over the entrance door, and a plan laid to throw the whole of it over me as I should pass out of the house, of all which my friends and I were unaware. After I bad been driven from the pulpit by the unsalable eggs, which were thrown about very freely, I stopped in the body of the church to discuss a single point with one of the respectable rowdies, when the audience became silent, and I went on and spoke above an hour, all the while receiving the strictest attention from every one present. At the conclusion the lights were put out, and preparation made to flour me over, although I had evidently changed the opinions of many of their company. As we were jamming along towards the door, one of the mob whispered to me,

"They are going to throw a bag of flour on you; so when you hear any one say, 'Let it slide,' you look out." Thus on my guard, and in possession of their signal, I determined to have a little fun at their expense. Therefore, when some of the best dressed and most respectable looking of their own company, or those who had no sympathy with my mission, filled up the doorway, I cried out in a disguised voice, "Let it slide;" and down came the contents of the bag, to the delight of my friends and the consternation of the enemy. A quarrel arose among the men at the door, and while they were settling their difficulty, my few friends and I quietly walked away unharmed.

Invited by influential English abolitionists, and elected a delegate to the Peace Congress at Paris, I sailed for Liverpool in the Royal Mail Steamship Canada, in the month of July, 1849. The passage was pleasant, and we arrived out in less than ten days.

I visited Dublin, where I partook of the hospitality of Richard D. Webb, Esq., and went from there to London; thence to Paris, to discharge the duties of my mission on peace.

In the French capital I met some of the most noted of the English philanthropists, who were also there in attendance on the Congress--Joseph Sturge, Richard Cobden, and men of that class.

Returning to London after the adjournment of the peace gathering, I was invited to various parts of the United Kingdom, and remained abroad a little more than five years, during which time I wrote and published three books, lectured in every town of any note in England,Ireland, Scotland, and Wales, besides visiting the Continent four times.

Anxious to be again in my native land, battling the monster Slavery, I returned home to America in the autumn of 1854; since which time I have travelled the length and breadth of the free states.

From the Scotch Independent, June 20,1852.

# WILLIAM WELLS BROWN.

ONE of the best arguments against the institution of slavery in America, and in favor of letting the African and his descendants go free, is to be found in the natural genius, manly courage, and ability exhibited by specimens of the race which have come to us from the other side of the Atlantic. Our citizens have not forgotten the visit of Mr. William Wells Brown, who so charmed them with his eloquent addresses on that occasion. But it is not on the platform that this gentleman makes the best show of talent. We have just received his "Three Years in Europe," and it is as a writer that he creates the most profound sensation.

He is no ordinary man, or he could not have so remarkably surmounted the many difficulties and impediments of his training as a slave. By dint of resolution, self-culture, and force of character, he has rendered himself a popular lecturer to a British audience, and vigorous expositor of the evils and atrocities of that system whose chains he has shaken off so triumphantly and forever. We may safely pronounce William Wells Brown a remarkable man, and a full refutation of the doctrine of the inferiority of the negro.

This is an interesting volume, ably written, bearing on every page the impress of honest purpose and noble aspiration. One is amused by the well-told anecdotes, and charmed with the painter-like descriptions of towns, cities, and natural scenery. Indeed, our author gives many very recognizable sketches of the places he has seen and people he has met.

We are not alone in our high estimation of the author's abilities, for we observe that the press of this country is unanimous in its praise of his book. The Literary Gazette, an excellent authority, says of it,--

"The appearance of this book is too remarkable a literary event to pass without a notice. At the moment when attention in this country is directed to the state of the colored people in America, the book appears with additional advantage; if nothing else were attained by its publication, it is well to have another proof of the capability of the negro intellect. Altogether, Mr. Brown has written a pleasing and amusing volume, and we are glad to bear this testimony to the literary merit of a work by a negro author."

The Eclectic Review, edited by the venerable Dr. Price, one of the best critics in the realm, has the following :--

"Though he never had a day's schooling in his life, he has produced a literary work not unworthy of a highly-educated gentleman. Our readers will find in these letters much instruction, not a little entertainment, and the beatings of a manly heart, on behalf of a down-trodden race, with which they will not fail to sympathize."

The Rev. Dr. Campbell, in the British Banner, devotes nearly two columns to Mr. Brown and his work, and concludes in these words:--

"We have read this book with an unusual measure of interest. Seldom, indeed, have we met with anything more captivating. It somehow happens that all these fugitive slaves are persons of superior talents. The pith of the volume consists in narratives of voyages and journeys made by the author in England, Scotland, Ireland, and France; and we can assure our readers that Mr. Brown has travelled to some purpose. The number of white men is not great who could have made more of the many things that came before them. There is in the work a vast amount of quotable matter, which, but for want of space, we should be glad to extract. As the volume, however, is published with a view to promote the benefit of the interesting fugitive, we deem it better to give it general opinion, by which curiosity may be whetted, than to gratify it by large citation. A book more worth the money has not, for a considerable time, come into our hands."

And even a word of cheer comes to the author from Printing-House Square, for The Times reviews the book, and says,--

"He writes with ease and ability, and his intelligent observations upon the great question to which he has devoted and is devoting his life will be read with interest, kind will command influence and respect."

If this be a fair representative of the American slaves, (and we see no reason to doubt it,) the sooner that our trans-Atlantic cousins abolish their hateful system, the better it will be for the character of those who profess to love Christ, and to live up to his precepts. Such men as William Wells Brown, Frederick Douglass, and the Rev. Alexander Crummell, will lose nothing by a comparison with the best educated and most highly cultivated of the Anglo-Saxons. We are also glad to see that his refinements and talents are appreciated by the literary circles of London; for we observed his name among the list of notables at a party given by Mr. Charles Dickens, on the 20th inst. Such treatment will encourage him, while it will at the same time rebuke that spirit of caste, on the other side of the ocean, which excludes from society the man of true merit on account of his color.

## THE BLACK MAN AND HIS ANTECEDENTS.

OF the great family of man, the negro has, during the last half century, been more prominently before the world than any other race. He did not seek this notoriety. Isolated away in his own land, he would have remained there, had it not been for the avarice of other races, who sought him out as a victim of slavery. Two and a half centuries of the negro's enslavement have created, in many minds, the opinion that he is intellectually inferior to the rest of mankind; and now that the blacks seem in a fair way to get their freedom in this country, it has been asserted, and from high authority in the government, that the natural inferiority of the negro makes it impossible for him to live on this continent with the white man, unless in a state of bondage.

In his interview with a committee of the colored citizens of the District of Columbia, on the 14th of August last, the President of the United States intimated that the whites and the blacks could not live together in peace, on account of one race being superior intellectually to the other. Mr. Postmaster General Blair, in his letter to the Union mass meeting held at the Cooper Institute, in New York, in March last, takes this ground. The Boston "Post" and "Courier" both take the same position.

I admit that the condition of my race, whether considered in a mental, moral, or intellectual point of view, at the present time cannot compare favorably with the Anglo-Saxon. But it does not become the whites to point the finger of scorn at the blacks, when they have so long been degrading them. The negro has not always been considered the inferior race. The time was when he stood at the head of science and literature. Let us see.

It is the generally received opinion of the most eminent historians and ethnologists, that the Ethiopians were really negroes, although in them the physical characteristics of the race were exhibited in a less marked manner than in those dwelling on the coast of Guinea, from whence the stock or American slaves has been chiefly derived. That, in the earliest periods of history, the Ethiopians had attained a high degree of civilization, there is every reason to believe; and that to the learning and science derived from them we must ascribe those wonderful monuments which still exist to attest the power and skill of the ancient Egyptians.

Among those who favor this opinion is our own distinguished countryman, Alexander H. Everett, and upon this evidence I base my argument. Volney assumes it as a settled point that the Egyptians were black. Herodotus, who travelled extensively through that interesting land, set them down as black, with curled hair, and having the negro features. The sacred writers were aware of their complexion: hence the question, "Can the Ethiopian change his skin?" The image of the negro is engraved upon the monuments of Egypt, not as a bondman, but as the master of art. The Sphinx, one of the wonders of the world, surviving the wreck of centuries, exhibits these same features at the present day. Minerva, the goddess of wisdom, was supposed to have been an African princess. Atlas, whose shoulders sustained the globe, and even the great Jupiter Ammon himself, were located by the mythologists in Africa. Though there may not be much in these fables, they teach us, nevertheless, who were then considered the nobles of the human race. Euclid, Homer, and Plato were Ethiopians. Terence, the most refined and accomplished scholar of his time, was of the same race. Hanno, the father of Hamilear, and grandfather of Hannibal, was a negro. These are the antecedents of the enslaved blacks on this continent.

From whence sprang the Anglo-Saxon? For, mark you, it is he that denies the equality of the negro. "When the Britons first became known to the Tyrian mariners," says Macaulay, "they were little superior to the Sandwich Islanders."

Hume says they were a rude and barbarous people, divided into numerous tribes, dressed in the skins of wild beasts. Druidism was their religion, and they were very superstitious. Such is the first account we have of the Britons. When the Romans invaded that country, they reduced the people to a state of vassalage as degrading as that of slavery in the Southern States. Their king, Caractacus, was captured and sent a slave to Rome. Still later, Hengist and Horsa, the Saxon generals, presented another yoke, which the Britons wore compelled to wear. But the last dregs of the bitter cup of humiliation were drunk when William of Normandy met Harold at Hastings, and, with a single blow, completely annihilated the nationality of the Britons. Thousands of the conquered people were then sent to the slave markets of Rome, where they were sold very cheap on account of their inaptitude to learn.

This is not very flattering to the President's ancestors, but it is just. Cæsar, in writing home, said of the Britons, "They are the most ignorant people I ever conquered. They cannot be taught music." Cicero, writing to his friend Atticus, advised him not to buy slaves from England, "because," said he, "they cannot be taught to read, and are the ugliest and most stupid race I ever saw." I am sorry that Mr. Lincoln came from such a low origin; but he is not to blame. I only find fault with him for making mouths at me.

"You should not the ignorant negro despise;

Just such your sires appeared in Cæsar's eyes."

The Britons lost their nationality, became amalgamated with the Romans, Saxons, and Normans, and out of this conglomeration sprang the proud Anglo-Saxon of to-day. I once stood upon the walls of an English city, built by enslaved Britons when Julius Cæsar was their master. The image of the ancestors of President Lincoln and Montgomery Blair, as represented in Britain, was carved upon the monuments of Rome, where they may still be seen in their chains. Ancestry is something which the white American should not speak of, unless with his lips to the dust.

"Nothing," says Macaulay, "in the early existence of Britain, indicated the greatness which she was destined to attain." Britain has risen, while proud Rome, Once the mistress of the world, has fallen; but the image of the early Englishman in his chains, as carved twenty centuries ago, is still to be seen upon her broken monuments. So has Egypt fallen ; and her sable sons and daughters have been scattered into nearly every land where the white man has introduced slavery and disgraced the soil with his footprint. As I gazed upon the beautiful and classic obelisk of Luxor, removed from Thebes, where it had stood four thousand years, and transplanted to the Place de la Concorde, at Paris, and contemplated its hieroglyphic inscription of the noble daring of Sesostris, the African general, who drew kings at his chariot wheels, and left monumental inscriptions from Ethiopia to India, I felt proud of my antecedents, proud of the glorious past, which no amount of hate and prejudice could wipe from history's page, while I had to mourn over the fall and the degradation of my race. But I do not despair; for the negro has that intellectual genius which God has planted in the mind of man, that distinguishes him from the rest of creation, and which needs only cultivation to make it bring forth fruit. No nation has ever been found, which, by its own unaided efforts, by some powerful inward impulse, has arisen from barbarism and degradation to civilization and respectability. There is nothing in race or blood, in color or features, that imparts susceptibility of improvement to one race over another. The mind left to itself from infancy, without culture, remains a blank. Knowledge is not innate. Development makes the man. As the Greeks, and Romans, and Jews drew knowledge from the Egyptians three thousand years ago, and the Europeans received it from the Romans, so must the blacks of this land rise in the same way. As one man learns from another, so nation learns from nation. Civilization is handed from one people to another, its great fountain and source being God our Father. No one, in the days of Cicero and Tacitus, could have predicted that the barbarism and savage wildness of the Germans would give place to the learning, refinement, and culture which that people now exhibit. Already the blacks on this continent, though kept down under the heel of the white man, are fast rising in the scale of intellectual development, and proving their equality with the brotherhood of man.

In his address before the Colonization Society, at Washington, on the 18th of January, 1853, Hon. Edward Everett said, "When I lived in Cambridge, a few years ago, I used to attend, as one of the board of visitors, the examinations of a classical school, in which was a colored boy, the son of a slave in Mississippi, I think. He appeared to me to be of pure African blood. There were at the same time two youths from Georgia, and one of my own sons, attending the same school. I must say that this poor negro boy, Beverly Williams, was one of the best scholars at the school, and in the Latin language he was the best scholar in his class. There are others, I am told, which show still more conclusively the aptitude of the colored race for every kind of intellectual culture."

Mr. Everett cited several other instances which had fallen under his notice, and utterly scouted the idea that there was any general inferiority of the African race. He said, "They have done as well as persons of European or Anglo-American origin would have done, after three thousand years of similar depression and hardship. The question has been asked, 'Does not the negro labor under some incurable, natural inferiority?' In this, for myself, I have no belief."

I think that this is ample refutation of the charge of the natural inferiority of the negro. President Lincoln, in the interview to which I have already referred, said, "But for your race among us there would not be a war." This reminds me of an incident that occurred while travelling in the State of Ohio, in 1844. Taking the stage coach at a small village, one of the passengers (a white man) objected to my being allowed a seat inside, on account of my color. I persisted, however, in claiming the right which my ticket gave me, and got in. The objector at once took a seat on a trunk on the top of the coach. The wire netting round the top of the stage not being strong, the white passenger, trunks and all, slid off as we were going down a steep hill. The top passenger's shoulder was dislocated, and in his pain he cried out, "If you had not been black, I should not have left my seat inside."

The "New York Herald," the "Boston Post," the "Boston Courier," and the "New York Journal of Commerce," take the lead in misrepresenting the effect which emancipation in the West Indies had upon the welfare of those islands. It is asserted that general ruin followed the black man's liberation. As to the British colonies, the fact is well established that slavery had impoverished the soil, demoralized the people, bond and free, brought the planters to a state of bankruptcy, and all the islands to ruin, long before Parliament had passed the act of emancipation. All the colonies, including Jamaica, had petitioned the home government for assistance, ten years prior to the liberation of their slaves. It is a noticeable fact, that the free blacks were the least embarrassed, in a pecuniary point of view, and that they appeared in more comfortable circumstances than the whites. There was a large proportion of free blacks in each of the colonies, Jamaica alone having fifty-five thousand before the day of emancipation. A large majority of the West India estates were owned by persons residing in Europe, and who had never seen the colonies. These plantations were carried on by agents, overseers, and clerks, whose mismanagement, together with the blighting influence which chattel slavery takes with it wherever it goes, brought the islands under impending ruin, and many of the estates were mortgaged in Europe for more than their value. One man alone, Neil Malcomb, of London, had forty plantations to fall upon his hands for money advanced on them before the abolition of slavery. These European proprietors, despairing of getting any returns from the West Indies, gladly pocketed their share of the twenty million pounds sterling, which the home government gave them, and abandoned their estates to their ruin. Other proprietors residing in the colonies formed combinations to make the emancipated people labor for scarcely enough to purchase food for them. If found idle, the tread-wheel, the chain-gang, the dungeon, with black bread, and water from the moat, and other modes of legalized torture, were inflicted upon the negroes. Through the determined and combined efforts of the land owners, the condition of the freed people was as bad, if not worse, for the first three years after their liberation, than it was before. Never was all experiment more severely tested than that of emancipation in the West Indies.

Nevertheless, the principles of freedom triumphed; not a drop of blood was shed by the enfranchised blacks; the colonies have arisen from the blight which they labored under in the time of slavery; the land has increased in value; and, above all, that which is more valuable than cotton, sugar, or rice--the moral and intellectual condition of both blacks and whites is in a better state now than ever before. Sir William Colebrook, governor of Antigua, said, six years after the islands were freed, "At the lowest computation, the land, without a single slave upon it, is fully as valuable now as it was, including all the slaves, before emancipation." In a report made to the British Parliament, in 1859, it was stated that three fifths of the cultivated land of Jamaica was the bona fide property of the blacks. The land is in a better state of cultivation now than it was while slavery existed, and both imports and exports show a great increase. Every thing, demonstrates that emancipation in the West India islands has resulted in the most satisfactory manner, and fulfilled the expectation of the friends of freedom throughout the world.

Rev. Mr. Underhill, secretary of the English Baptist Missionary Society, who has visited Jamaica, and carefully studied its condition, said, in a recent speech in London, that the late slaves in that island had built some two hundred and twenty chapels. The churches that worship in them number fifty-three thousand communicants, amounting to one eighth of the total population. The average attendance, in other than the state churches, is ninety-one thousand--a fourth of the population. One third of the children-- twenty-two thousand--are in the schools. The blacks voluntarily contribute twenty-two thousand pounds (one hundred and ten thousand dollars) annually for religious purposes. Their landed property exceeds five million dollars. Valuing their cottages at only fifty dollars each, these amount to three million dollars. They have nearly three hundred thousand dollars deposited in the savings banks. The sum total of their property is much above eleven million dollars. All this has been accumulated since their emancipation.

Thus it is seen that all parties have been benefited by the abolition of negro slavery in the British possessions. Now we turn to our own land. Among the many obstacles which have been brought to bear against emancipation, one of the most formidable has been the series of objections urged against it upon what has been supposed to be the slave's want of appreciation of liberty, and his ability to provide for himself in a state of freedom; and now that slavery seems to be near its end, these objections are multiplying, and the cry is heard all over the land, "What shall be done with the slave if freed?"

It has been clearly demonstrated, I think, that the enslaved of the south are as capable of self-support as any other class of people in the country. It is well known that, throughout the entire south, a large class of slaves have been for years accustomed to hire their time from their owners. Many of these have paid very high prices for the privilege. Some able mechanics have been known to pay as high as six hundred dollar per annum, besides providing themselves with food and clothing; and this class of slaves, by their industry, have taken care of themselves so well, and their appearance has been so respectable, that many of the states have passed laws prohibiting masters from letting their slaves out to themselves, because, as it was said, it made the other slaves dissatisfied to see so many of their fellows well provided, and accumulating something for themselves in the way of pocket money.

The Rev. Dr. Nehemiah Adams, whose antecedents have not been such as to lead to the suspicion that he favors the free colored men, or the idea of giving to the slaves their liberty, in his "South-Side View," unconsciously and unintentionally gives a very valuable statement upon this particular point. Dr. Adams says, "A slave woman having had three hundred dollars stolen from her by a white man, her master was questioned in court as to the probability of her having had so much money. The master said that he not unfrequently had borrowed fifty and a hundred dollars from her himself, and added that she was always very strict as to his promised time of payment." There was a slave woman who had not only kept every agreement with her master--paying him every cent she had promised--but had accumulated three hundred dollars towards purchasing her liberty ; and it was stolen from her, not by a black man, but, as Dr. Adams says, by a white man.

But one of the clearest demonstrations of the ability of the slave to provide for himself in a state of freedom is to be found in the prosperous condition of the large free colored population of the Southern States. Maryland has eighty thousand, Virginia seventy thousand, and the other slave states have a large number. These free people have all been slaves, or they are the descendants of those who were once slaves; what they have gained has been acquired in spite of the public opinion and laws of the south, in spite of prejudice, and every thing. They have acquired a large amount of property; and it is this industry, this sobriety, this intelligence, and this wealth of the free colored people the south, that has created so much prejudice on the part of slaveholders against them. They have felt that the very presence of a colored man, looking so genteelly and in such a prosperous condition, made the slaves unhappy and discontented. In the Southern Rights Convention which assembled at Baltimore, June 8, 1860, a resolution was adopted, calling on the legislature to pass a law driving the free colored people out of the state. Nearly every speaker took the ground that the free colored people must be driven out to make the slave's obedience more secure. Judge Mason, in his speech, said, "It is the thrifty and well-to-do free negroes, that are seen by our slaves, that make them dissatisfied." A similar appeal was made to the legislature of Tennessee. Judge Catron, of the

Supreme Court of the United States, in a long and able letter to the Nashville "Union," opposed the driving out of the colored people. He said they were among the best mechanics, the best artisans, and the most industrious laborers in the state, and that to drive them, out would be an injury to the state itself. This is certainly good evidence in their behalf.

The New Orleans "True Delta" opposed the passage of a similar law by the State of Louisiana. Among other things it said, "There are a large free colored population here, correct in their general deportment, honorable in their intercourse with society, and free from reproach so far as the laws are concerned, not surpassed in the inoffensiveness of their lives by any equal number of persons in any place, north or south."

A movement was made in the legislature of South Carolina to expel the free blacks from that state, and a committee was appointed to investigate the matter. In their report the committee said, "We find that the free blacks of this state are among our most industrious people; in this city (Charleston) we find that they own over two and a half millions of dollars worth of property; that they pay two thousand seven hundred dollars tax to the city."

Dr. Nehemiah Adams, whom I have already quoted, also testifies to the good character of the free colored people; but he does it unintentionally; it was not a part of the programme; how it slipped in I cannot tell. Here it is, however, from page 41 of his "South-Side View:"--

"A prosecuting officer, who had six or eight counties in his district, told me that, during eight years service, he had made out about two thousand bills of indictment, of which not more than twelve were against colored persons."

Hatred of the free colored people, and abuse of them, have always been popular with the pro-slavery people of this country; yet, an American senator from one of the Western States--a man who never lost an opportunity to vilify and traduce the colored man, and who, in his last canvass for a seat in the United States Senate, argued that the slaves were better off in slavery than they would be if set free, and declared that the blacks were unable to take care of themselves while enjoying liberty--died, a short time since, twelve thousand dollars in debt to a black man, who was the descendant of a slave.

There is a Latin phrase--De mortuis nil nisi bonum. It is not saying any thing against the reputation of Hon. Stephen A. Douglas to tell the fact that he had borrowed money from a negro. I only find fault with him that he should traduce the class that befriended him in the time of need. James Gordon Bennett, of the New York Herald, in a time of great pecuniary distress, soon after establishing his paper, borrowed three hundred dollars of a black man; and now he is one of our most relentless enemies. Thus it is that those who fattened upon us often turn round and traduce us: Reputation is, indeed, dear to every nation and race; but to us, the colored people of this country, who have so many obstacles to surmount, it is doubly dear:--

> "Who steals my purse steals trash;
> 'Twas mine, 'tis his, and has been slave to thousands;
> But he who filches from me my good name,
> Robs me of that which not enriches him,
> And makes me poor indeed."

You know we were told by the slaveholders, before the breaking out of the rebellion, that if we got into any difficulty with the south, their slaves would take up arms and fight to a man for them. Mr. Toombs, I believe, threatened that he would arm his slaves, and other men in Congress from the slave states made the same threat. They were going to arm the slaves and turn them against the north. They said they could be trusted; and many people here at the north really believed that the slave did not want his liberty, would not have it if he could, and that the slave population was a very dangerous element against the north; but at once, on the approach of our soldiers, the slaves are seen, with their bundles and baskets, and hats and coats, and without bundles or baskets, and without hats or coats, rushing to our lines; demonstrating what we have so often said, that all the slave was waiting for was the opportunity to get his liberty. Why should you not have believed this? Why should you have supposed for a moment, that, because a man's color differs a little from yours, he is better contented to remain a slave than you would be, or that he has no inclination, no wish, to escape from the thraldom that holds him so tight? What is it that does not wish to be free?

"Go, let a cage with grates of gold,
And pearly roof, the eagle hold;
Let dainty viands be its fare,
And give the captive tenderest care;
But say, in luxury's limits pent,
Find you the king of birds content?
No; oft he'll sound the startling shriek,
And dash the cage with angry beak:
Precarious freedom's far more dear
Than all the prison's pampering cheer."

As with the eagle, so with man. He loves to look upon the bright day and the stormy night; to gaze upon the broad, free ocean, its eternal surging tides, its mountain billows, and its foam-crested waves; to tread the steep mountain side; to sail upon the placid river; to wander along the gurgling stream ; to trace the sunny slope, the beautiful landscape, the majestic forest, the flowery meadow; to listen to the howling of the winds and the music of the birds. These are the aspirations of man, without regard to country, clime, or color.

"What shall we do with the slave of the south? Expatriate him," say the haters of the negro. Expatriate him for what? He has cleared up the swamps of the south, and has put the soil under cultivation; he has built up her towns, and cities, and villages; he has enriched the north and Europe with his cotton, and sugar, and rice; and for this you would drive him out of the country! "What shall be done with the slaves if they are freed?" You had better ask "What shall we do with the slaveholders if the slaves are freed?" The slave has shown himself better fitted to take care of himself than the slaveholder. He is the bone and sinew of the south; he is the producer, while the master is nothing but a consumer, and a very poor consumer at that. The slave is the producer, and he alone can be relied upon. He has the sinew, the determination, and the will; and if you will take the free colored people of the south as the criterion, take their past history as a sample of what the colored people are capable of doing, every one must be satisfied that the slaves can take care of themselves. Some say, "Let them alone; they are well cared for, and that is enough."

"O, tell us not they're clothed and fed--
'Tis insult, stuff, and a' that;
With freedom gone, all joy is fled,
For Heaven's best gift is a' that."

But it is said, "The two races cannot live together in a state of freedom." Why, that is the cry that rung all over England thirty years ago: "If you liberate the slaves of the West Indies, they can't live with the whites in a state of freedom." Thirty years have shown the contrary. The blacks and the whites live together in Jamaica; they are all prosperous, and the island in a better condition than it ever was before the act of emancipation was passed.

But they tell us, "If the slaves are emancipated, we won't receive them upon an equality." Why, every man must make equality for himself. No society, no government, can make this equality. I do not expect the slave of the south to jump into equality; all I claim for him is, that he may be allowed to jump into liberty, and let him make equality for himself. I have some white neighbors around me in Cambridge; they are not very intellectual; they don't associate with my family; but whenever they shall improve themselves, and bring themselves up by their own intellectual and moral worth, I shall not object to their coming into my society--all things being equal.

Now, this talk about not letting a man come to this place or that, and that we won't do this for him, or won't do that for him, is all idle. The anti-slavery agitators have never demanded that you shall take the colored man, any more than that you shall take the uncultivated and uncouth white man, and place him in a certain position in society. All I demand for the black man is, that the white people shall take their heels off his neck, and let him have a chance to rise by his own efforts.

The idea of colonizing the slaves in some other country, outside of the United States, seems the height of folly. Whatever may be the mineral wealth of a country, or the producing capabilities of the soil, neither can be made available without the laborer. Four millions of strong hands cannot be spared from the Southern States. All time has shown that the negro is the best laborer in the tropics.

The slaves once emancipated and left on the lands, four millions of new consumers will spring into existence. Heretofore, the bondmen have consumed nothing scarcely from the north. The cost of keeping a slave was only about nineteen dollars per annum, including food, clothing, and doctors' bills. Negro cloth, negro shoes, and negro whips were all that were sent south by northern manufacturers. Let slavery be abolished, and stores will be opened and a new trade take place with the blacks south. Northern manufacturers will have to run on extra time till this new demand will have been supplied. The slave owner, having no longer an inducement to be idle, will go to work, and will not have time to concoct treason against the stars and stripes. I cannot close this appeal without a word about the free blacks in the non-slaveholding states.

The majority of the colored people in the Northern States descended from slaves: many of the were slaves themselves. In education, in morals, and in the development of mechanical genius, the free blacks of the Northern States will compare favorably with any laboring class in the world. And considering the fact that we have been shut out, by a cruel prejudice, from nearly all the mechanical branches, and all the professions, it is marvellous that we have attained the position we now occupy. Notwithstanding those bars, our young men have learned trades, become artists, gone into the professions, although bitter prejudice may prevent their having a great deal of practice. When it is considered that they have mostly come out of bondage, and that their calling has been the lowest kind in every community, it is still more strange that the colored people have amassed so much wealth in every state in the Union. If this is not an exhibition of capacity, I don't understand the meaning of the term. And if true patriotism and devotion to the cause of freedom be tests of loyalty, and should establish one's claim to all the privileges that the government can confer, then surely the black man can demand his rights with a good grace. From the fall of Attucks, the first martyr of the American revolution in 1770, down to the present day, the colored people have shown themselves worthy of any confidence that the nation can place in its citizens in the time that tries men's souls. At the battle of Bunker Hill, on the heights of Groton, at the ever-memorable battle of Red Bank, the sable sons of our country stood side by side with their white brethren. On Lakes Erie and Champlain, on the Hudson, and down in the valley of the Mississippi, they established their valor and their invincibility. Whenever the rights of the nation have been assailed, the negro has always responded to his country's call, at once, and with every pulsation of his heart beating for freedom. And no class of Americans have manifested more solicitude for the success of the federal arms in the present struggle with rebellion, than the colored people. At the north, they were among the earliest to respond to the president's first proclamation, calling for troops. At the south, they have ever shown a preference for the stars and stripes. In his official despatch to Minister Adams, Mr. Secretary Seward said,--

"Every where the American general receives his most useful and reliable information from the negro, who hails his coming as the harbinger of freedom."
THE BLACK MAN,HIS GENIUS AND HIS ACHIEVEMENTS.

# BENJAMIN BANNEKER.

THE services rendered to science, to liberty, and to the intellectual character of the negro by Banneker, are too great for us to allow his name to sleep and his genius and merits to remain hidden from the world. BENJAMIN BANNEKER was born in the State of Maryland, in the year 1732, of pure African parentage; their blood never having been corrupted by the introduction of a drop of Anglo-Saxon. His father was a slave, and of course could do nothing towards the education of the child. The mother, however, being free, succeeded in purchasing the freedom of her husband, and they, with their son, settled on a few acres of land, where Benjamin remained during the lifetime of his parents. His entire schooling was gained from an obscure country school, established for the education of the children of free negroes; and these advantages were poor, for the boy appears to have finished studying before be arrived at his fifteenth year. Although out of school, Banneker was still a student, and read with great care and attention such books as he could get. Mr. George Ellicott, a gentleman of fortune and considerable literary taste, and who resided near to Benjamin, became interested in him, and lent him books from his large library. Among these books were Mayer's Tables, Fergusson's Astronomy, and Leadbeater's Lunar Tables. A few old and imperfect astronomical instruments also found their way into the boy's hands, all of which he used with great benefit to his own mind.

Banneker took delight in the study of the languages, and soon mastered the Latin, Greek, and German. He was also proficient in the French. The classics were not neglected by him, and the general literary knowledge which he possessed caused Mr. Ellicott to regard him as the most learned man in the town, and he never failed to introduce Banneker to his most distinguished guests. About this time Benjamin turned his attention particularly to astronomy, and determined on making calculations for an almanac, and completed a set for the whole year. Encouraged by this attempt, he entered upon calculations for subsequent years, which, as well as the former, he began and finished without the least assistance from any person or books than those already mentioned; so that whatever merit is attached to his performance is exclusively his own. He published an almanac in Philadelphia for the years 1792, '3, '4, and '5, which contained his calculations, exhibiting the different aspects of the planets, a table of the motions of the sun and moon, their risings and settings, and the courses of the bodies of the planetary system. By this time Banneker's acquirements had become generally known, and the best scholars in the country opened correspondence with him. Goddard & Angell, the well-known Baltimore publishers, engaged his pen for their establishment, and became the publishers of his almanacs. A copy of his first production was sent to Thomas Jefferson, together with a letter intended to interest the great statesman in the cause of negro emancipation and the elevation of the race, in which he says,--

"It is a truth too well attested to need a proof here, that we are a race of beings who have long labored under the abuse and censure of the world; that we have long been looked upon with an eye of contempt and considered rather as brutish than human, and scarcely capable of mental endowments. I hope I may safely admit, in consequence of the report which has reached me, that you are a man far less inflexible in sentiments of this nature than many others; that you are measurably friendly and well disposed towards us, and that you are willing to lend your aid and assistance for our relief from those many distresses and numerous calamities to which we are reduced. If this is founded in truth, I apprehend you will embrace every opportunity to eradicate that train of absurd and false ideas and opinions which so generally prevail with respect to us, and that your sentiments are concurrent with mine, which are, that one universal Father hath given being to us all; that he hath not only made us all of one flesh, but that he hath also, without partiality, afforded us all the same sensations, and endowed us all with the same faculties; and that, however variable we may be in society or religion, however diversified in situation or in color, we are all of the same family, and stand in the same relation to him. If these are sentiments of which you are fully persuaded, you cannot but acknowledge that it is the indispensable duty of those who maintain the rights of human nature, and who profess the obligations of Christianity, to extend their power and influence to the relief of every part of the human race from whatever burden or oppression they may unjustly labor under; and this, I apprehend, a full conviction of the truth and obligation of these principles should lead all to. I have long been convinced that if your love for yourselves, and for those inestimable laws which preserved to you the rights of human nature, was founded on sincerity, you could not but be solicitous that every individual, of whatever rank or distinction, might with you equally enjoy the blessings thereof; neither could you rest satisfied short of the most active effusion of your exertions, in order to effect their promotion from any state of degradation to which the unjustifiable cruelty and barbarism of men may have reduced them.

"I freely and cheerfully acknowledge that I am one of the African race, and in that color which is natural to them, of the deepest dye; and it is under a sense of the most profound gratitude to the Supreme Ruler of the universe, that I now confess to you that I am not under that state of tyrannical thraldom and inhuman captivity to which too many of my brethren are doomed; but that I have abundantly tasted of the fruition of those blessings which proceed from that free and unequalled liberty with which you are favored, and which I hope you will willingly allow you have mercifully received from the immediate hand of that Being from whom proceedeth every good and perfect gift.

"Your knowledge of the situation of my brethren is too extensive to need a recital here; neither shall I presume to prescribe methods by which they may be relieved, otherwise than by recommending to you and to others to wean yourselves from those narrow prejudices which you have imbibed with respect to them, and, as Job proposed to his friends, 'put your soul in their souls' stead.' Thus shall your hearts be enlarged with kindness and benevolence towards them; and thus shall you need neither the direction of myself or others in what manner to proceed herein. . . . The calculation for this almanac is the production of my arduous study in my advanced stage of life; for having long had unbounded desires to become acquainted with the secrets of nature, I have had to gratify my curiosity herein through my own assiduous application to astronomical study, in which I need not recount to you the many difficulties and disadvantages which I have had to encounter."

Mr. Jefferson at once replied as follows:--

"PHILADELPHIA, August 30, 1791.

"SIR: I thank you sincerely for your letter and the almanac it contained. Nobody wishes more than I do to see such proofs as you exhibit, that nature has given to our black brethren talents equal to those of the other colors of men, and that the appearance of the want of them is owing merely to the degraded condition of their existence, both in Africa and America. I can add with truth, that nobody wishes more ardently to see a good system commenced for raising their condition, both of their body and their mind, to what it ought to be, as far as the imbecility of their present existence, and other circumstances, which cannot be neglected, will admit. I have taken the liberty of sending your almanac to Monsieur de Condorcet, secretary of the Academy of Sciences at Paris, and a member of the Philanthropic Society, because I consider it as a document to which your whole color have a right for their justification against the doubts which have been entertained of them.

"I am, with great esteem,

"Dear sir, your obedient, &c.,

"THOMAS JEFFERSON.

"To MR. B. BANNEKER."

The letter from Banneker, together with the almanac, created in the heart of Mr. Jefferson a fresh feeling of enthusiasm in behalf of freedom, and especially for the negro, which ceased only with his life. The American statesman wrote to Brissot, the celebrated French writer, in which he made enthusiastic mention of the "Negro Philosopher." At the formation of the "Society of the Friends of the Blacks," at Paris, by Lafayette, Brissot, Barnave, Condorcet, and Gregoire, the name of Banneker was again and again referred to to prove the equality of the races. Indeed, the genius of the "Negro Philosopher" did much towards giving liberty to the people of St. Domingo. In the British House of Commons, Pitt, Wilberforce, and Buxton often alluded to Banneker by name, as a man fit to fill any position in society. At the setting off of the District of Columbia for the capital of the federal government, Banneker was invited by the Maryland commissioners, and took an honorable part in the settlement of the territory. But throughout all his intercourse with men of influence, he never lost sight of the condition of his race, and ever urged the emancipation and elevation of the slave. He well knew that every thing that was founded upon the admitted inferiority of natural right in the African was calculated to degrade him and bring him nearer to the foot of the oppressor, and he therefore never failed to allude to the equality of the races when with those whites whom he could influence. He always urged self-elevation upon the colored people whom he met. He felt that to deprive the black man of the inspiration of ambition, of hope, of health, of standing among his brethren of the earth, was to take from him all incentives to mental improvement. What husbandman incurs the toil of seed time and culture, except with a view to the subsequent enjoyment of a golden harvest? Banneker was endowed by nature with all those excellent qualifications which are necessary previous to the accomplishment of a great man. His memory was large and tenacious, yet, by a curious felicity chiefly susceptible of the finest impressions it received from the best authors he read, which he always preserved in their primitive strength and amiable order. He had a quickness of apprehension and a vivacity of understanding which easily took in and surmounted the most subtile and knotty parts of mathematics and metaphysics. He possessed in a large degree that genius which constitutes a man of letters; that quality without which judgment is cold and knowledge is inert; that energy which collects, combines, amplifies, and animates.

He knew every branch of history, both natural and civil, he had read all the original historians of England, France, and Germany, and was a great antiquarian. Criticism, metaphysics, morals, politics, voyages and travels, were all studied and well digested by him. With such a fund of knowledge his conversation was equally interesting, instructive, and entertaining. Banneker was so favorably appreciated by the first families in Virginia, that in 1803 he was invited by Mr. Jefferson, then President of the United States, to visit him at Monticello, where the statesman had gone for recreation. But he was too infirm to undertake the journey. He died the following year, aged seventy-two. Like the golden sun that has sunk beneath the western horizon, but still throws upon the world, which he sustained and enlightened in his career, the reflected beams of his departed genius, his name can only perish with his language.

Banneker believed in the divinity of reason, and in the omnipotence of the human understanding with Liberty for its handmaid. The intellect impregnated by science and multiplied by time, it appeared to him, must triumph necessarily over all the resistance of matter. He had faith in liberty, truth, and virtue. His remains still rest in the slave state where he lived and died, with no stone to mark the spot or tell that it is the grave of Benjamin Banneker.

He labored incessantly, lived irreproachably, and died in the literary harness, universally esteemed and regretted.

# NAT TURNER.

BIOGRAPHY is individual history, as distinguished from that of communities, of nations, and of worlds. Eulogy is that deserved applause which springs from the virtues and attaches itself to the characters of men. This is not intended either as a biography or a eulogy, but simply a sketch of one whose history has hitherto been neglected, and to the memory of whom the American people are not prepared to do justice.

On one of the oldest and largest plantations in in Southampton county, Virginia, owned by Benjamin Turner, Esq., Nat was born a slave, on the 2d of October, 1800. His parents were of unmixed African descent. Surrounded as he was by the superstition of the slave quarters, and being taught by his mother that he was born for a prophet, a preacher, and a deliverer of his race, it was not strange that the child should have imbibed the principles which were afterwards developed in his career. Early impressed with the belief that he had seen visions, and received communications direct from God, he, like Napoleon, regarded himself as a being of destiny. In his childhood Nat was of an amiable disposition; but circumstances in which he was placed as a slave, brought out incidents that created a change in his disposition, and turned his kind and docile feeling into the most intense hatred to the white race.

Being absent one night from his master's plantation without a pass, he was caught by Whitlock and Mull, the two district patrolers, and severely flogged. This act of cruelty inflamed the young slave, and he resolved upon having revenge. Getting two of the boys of a neighboring plantation to join him, Nat obtained a long rope, went out at night on the road through which the officers had their beat, and stationing his companions, one on each side of the road, he stretched the rope across, fastening each end to a tree, and drawing it tight. His rope thus fixed, and his accomplices instructed how to act their part, Nat started off up the road. The night being dark, and the rope only six or eight inches from the ground, the slave felt sure that he would give his enemies a "high fall."

Nat hearing them, he called out in a disguised voice, "Is dat you, Jim?" To this Whitlock replied, "Yes, dis is me." Waiting until the white men were near him, Nat started off upon a run, followed by the officers. The boy had placed a sheet of white paper in the road, so that he might know at what point to jump the rope, so as not to be caught in his own trap. Arriving at the signal he sprung over the rope, and went down the road like an antelope. But not so with the white men, for both were caught by the legs and thrown so hard upon the ground that Mull had his shoulder put out of joint, and his face terribly lacerated by the fall; while Whitlock's left wrist was broken, and his head bruised in a shocking manner. Nat hastened home, while his companions did the same, not forgetting to take with them the clothes line which had been so serviceable in the conflict. The patrolers were left on the field of battle, crying, swearing, and calling for help.

Snow seldom falls as far south as the southern part of Virginia; but when it does, the boys usually have a good time snow-balling, and on such occasions the slaves, old and young, women and men, are generally pelted without mercy, and with no right to retaliate. It was only a few months after his affair with the patrolers, that Nat was attacked by a gang of boys, who chased him some distance, snow-balling with all their power. The slave boy knew the lads, and determined upon revenge. Waiting till night, he filled his pockets with rocks, and went into the street. Very soon the same gang of boys were at his heels, and pelting him. Concealing his face so as not to be known, Nat discharged his rocks in every direction, until his enemies had all taken to their heels.

The ill treatment he experienced at the hands of the whites, and the visions be claimed to have seen, caused Nat to avoid, as far as he could, all intercourse with his follow-slaves, and threw around him a gloom and melancholy that disappeared only with his life.

Both the young slave and his friends averred that a full knowledge of the alphabet came to him in a single night. Impressed with the belief that his mission was a religious one, and this impression strengthened by the advice of his grandmother, a pious but ignorant woman, Nat commenced preaching when about twenty-five of age, but never went beyond his own master's locality. In stature he was under the middle size, long armed, round-shouldered, and strongly marked with the African features. A gloomy fire burned in his looks, and he had a melancholy expression of countenance. He never tasted a drop of ardent spirits all his life, and was never known to smile. In the year 1828 new visions appeared to Nat, and he claimed to have direct communication with God.

Unlike most of those born under the influence of slavery, he had no faith in conjuring, fortune-telling, or dreams, and always spoke with contempt of such things. Being hired out to cruel masters, he ran away, and remained in the woods thirty days, and could have easily escaped to the free states, as did his father some years before; but he received, as he says in his confession a communication from the spirit, which said, "Return to your earthly master, for he who knoweth his Master's will, and doeth it not, shall be beaten with many stripes." It was not the will of his earthly, but his heavenly Master that he felt bound to do, and therefore Nat returned. His follow-slaves were greatly incensed at him for coming back, for they knew well his ability to reach Canada, or some other land of freedom, if he was so inclined. He says further, "About this time I had a vision, and saw white spirits and black spirits engaged in battle, and the sun was darkened, the thunder rolled in the heavens, and blood flowed in streams; and I heard a voice saying, 'Such is your luck; such are you called on to see; and let it come, rough or smooth, you must surely bear it.'" Some time after this, Nat had, as he says, another vision, in which the spirit appeared and said, "The serpent is loosened, and Christ has laid down the yoke he has borne for the sins of men, and you must take it up, and fight against the serpent, for the time is fast approaching when the first shall be last, and the last shall be first." There is no doubt but that this last sentence filled Nat with enthusiastic feeling in favor of the liberty of his race, that he had so long dreamed of. "The last shall be first, and the first shall be last," seemed to him to mean something. He saw in it the overthrow of the whites, and the establishing of the blacks in their stead, and to this end he bent the energies of his mind. In February, 1831, Nat received his last communication, and beheld his last vision. He said, "I was told I should arise and prepare myself, and slay my enemies with their own weapons."

The plan of an insurrection was now formed in his own mind, and the time had arrived for him to take others into the secret; and he at once communicated his ideas to four of his friends, in whom he had implicit confidence. Hark Travis, Nelson Williams, Sam Edwards, and Henry Porter were slaves like himself, and like him had taken their names from their masters. A meeting must be held with these, and it must take place in some secluded place, where the whites would not disturb them; and a meeting was appointed. The spot where they assembled was as wild and romantic as were the visions that had been impressed upon the mind of their leader.

Three miles from where Nat lived was a dark swamp filled with reptiles, in the middle of which was a dry spot, reached by a narrow, winding path, and upon which human feet seldom trod, on account of its having been the place where a slave had been tortured to death by a slow fire, for the crime of having flogged his cruel and inhuman master. The night for the meeting arrived, and they came together. Hank brought a pig; Sam, bread; Nelson, sweet potatoes; and Henry, brandy; and the gathering was turned into a feast. Others were taken in, and joined the conspiracy. All partook heartily of the food and drank freely, except Nat. He fasted and prayed. It was agreed that the revolt should commence that night, and in their own master's households, and that each slave should give his oppressor the death blow. Before they left the swamp Nat made a speech, in which he said, "Friends and brothers: We are to commence a great work tonight. Our race is to be delivered from slavery, and God has appointed us as the men to do his bidding, and let us be worthy of our calling. I am told to slay all the whites we encounter, without regard to age or sex. We have no arms or ammunition, but we will find these in the houses of our oppressors, and as we go on others can join us. Remember that we do not go forth for the sake of blood and carnage, but it is necessary that in the commencement of this revolution all the whites we meet should die, until we shall have an army strong enough to carry on the war upon a Christian basis. Remember that ours is not a war for robbery and to satisfy our passions; it is a struggle for freedom. Ours must be deeds, and not words. Then let's away to the scene of action."

Among those who had joined the conspirators was Will, a slave, who scorned the idea of taking his master's name. Though his soul longed to be free, he evidently became one of the party, as much to satisfy revenge, as for the liberty that he saw in the dim distance. Will had seen a dear and beloved wife sold to the negro trader and taken away, never to be beheld by him again in this life. His own back was covered with scars, from his shoulders to his feet. A large scar, running from his right eye down to his chin, showed that he had lived with a cruel master. Nearly six feet in height, and one of the strongest and most athletic of his race, he proved to be the most unfeeling of all the insurrectionists. His only weapon was a broad-axe, sharp and heavy.

Nat and his accomplices at once started for the plantation of Joseph Travis, with whom the four lived, and there the first blow was struck. In his confession, just before his execution, Nat said,--

"On returning to the house, Hark went to the door with an axe, for the purpose of breaking it open, as we knew we were strong enough to murder the family should they be awakened by the noise; but reflecting that it might create an alarm in the neighborhood, we determined to enter the house secretly, and murder them whilst sleeping. Hark got a ladder and set it against the chimney, on which I ascended, and hoisting a window, entered and came down stairs, unbarred the doors, and removed the guns from their places. It was then observed that I must spill the first blood. On which, armed with a hatchet, and accompanied by Will, I entered my master's chamber. It being dark, I could not give a death blow. The hatchet glanced from his head; he sprang from the bed and called his wife. It was his last word; Will laid him dead with a blow of his axe, and Mrs. Travis shared the same fate, as she lay in bed. The murder of this family, five in number, was the work of a moment; not one of them awoke. There was a little infant sleeping in a cradle, that was forgotten until we had left the house and gone some distance, when Henry and Will returned and killed it. We got here four guns that would shoot, and several old muskets, with a pound or two of powder. We remained for some time at the barn, where we paraded; I formed them in line as soldiers, and after carrying them through all the manoeuvres I was master of, marched them off to Mr. Salathiel Francis's, about six hundred yards distant.

"Sam and Will went to the door and knocked. Mr. Francis asked who was there; Sam replied it was he, and he had a letter for him; on this he got up and came to the door; they immediately seized him and dragging him out a little from the door, he was despatched by repeated blows on the head. There was no other white person in the family. We started from there to Mrs. Reese's, maintaining the most perfect silence on our march, where, finding the door unlocked, we entered and murdered Mrs. Reese in her bed while sleeping; her son awoke, but only to sleep the sleep of death; he had only time to say, 'Who is that?' and he was no more. From Mrs. Reese's we went to Mrs. Turner's, a mile distant, which we reached about sunrise, on Monday morning. Henry, Austin, and Sam, went to the still, where, finding Mr. Peebles, Austin shot him; the rest of us went to the house. As we approached, the family discovered us and shut the door. Vain hope! Will, with one stroke of his axe, opened it, and we entered, and found Mrs. Turner and Mrs. Newsome in the middle of a room, almost frightened to death. Will immediately killed Mrs. Turner with one blow of his axe. I took Mrs. Newsome by the hand, and with the sword I had when apprehended, I struck her several blows over the head, but was not able to kill her, as the sword was dull. Will, turning round and discovering it, despatched her also. A general destruction of property, and search for money and ammunition, always succeeded the murders.

"By this time, my company amounted to fifteen, nine men mounted, who started for Mrs. Whitehead's, (the other six were to go through a by-way to Mr. Bryant's, and rejoin us at Mrs. Whitehead's.) As we approached the house we discovered Mr. Richard Whitehead standing in the cotton patch, near the lane fence; we called him over into the lane, and Will, the executioner, was near at hand, with his fatal axe, to send him to an untimely grave. As we pushed on to the house, I discovered some one running round the garden, and thinking it was some of the white family, I pursued, but finding it was a servant girl belonging to the house, I returned to commence the work of death; but they whom I left had not been idle: all the family were already murdered but Mrs. Whitehead and her daughter Margaret. As I came round to the door I saw Will pulling Mrs. Whitehead out of the house, and at the step he nearly severed her head from her body with his broadaxe. Miss Margaret, when I discovered her, had concealed herself in the corner formed by the projection of the cellar cap from the house; on my approach she fled, but was soon overtaken, and after repeated blows with a sword, I killed her by a blow over the head with a fence rail. By this time the six who had gone by Mr. Bryant's rejoined us, and informed me they had done the work of death assigned them. We again divided, part going to Mr. Richard Porter's, and from thence to Nathaniel Francis's, the others to Mr. Howell Harris's and Mr. T. Doyles's. On my reaching Mr. Porter's, he had escaped with his family. I understood there that the alarm had already spread, and I immediately returned to bring up those sent to Mr. Doyles's and Mr.Howell Harris's; the party I left going on to Mr. Francis's, having told them I would join them in that neighborhood. I met those sent to Mr. Doyles's and Mr. Howell Harris's returning, having met Mr. Doyles on the road and killed him. Learning from some who joined them, that Mr. Harris was from home, I immediately pursued the course taken by the party gone on before; but knowing that they would complete the work of death and pillage at Mr. Francis's before I could get there, I went to Mr. Peter Edwards's, expecting to find them there; but they had been there already. I then went to Mr. John T. Barrow's; they had been there and murdered him. I pursued on their track to Captain Newitt Harris's. I found the greater part mounted and ready to start; the men, now amounting to about forty, shouted and hurrahed as I rode up; some were in the yard loading their guns, others drinking. They said Captain Harris and his family had escaped; the property in the house they destroyed, robbing him of money and other valuables. I ordered them to mount and march instantly; this was about nine or ten o'clock, Monday morning. I proceeded to Mr. Levi Waller's, two or three miles distant. I took my station in the rear, and as it was my object to carry terror and devastation wherever we went, I placed fifteen or twenty of the best mounted and most to be relied on in front, who generally approached the houses as fast as their horses could run; this was for two purposes, to prevent their escape and strike terror to the inhabitants--on this account I never got to the houses, after leaving Mrs. Whitehead's, until the murders were committed, except in one case. I sometimes got in sight in time to see the work of death completed, viewed the mangled bodies as they lay, in silent satisfaction, and immediately started in quest of other victims. Having murdered Mrs. Waller and ten children, we started for Mr. William Williams's. We killed him and two little boys that were there; while engaged in this, Mrs. Williams fled, and got some distance from the house, but she was pursued, overtaken, and compelled to get up behind one of the company, who brought her back, and after showing her the mangled body of her lifeless husband, she was told to get down and lie by his side, where she was shot dead. I then started for Mr. Jacob Williams's, where the family were murdered. Here we found a young man named Drury, who had come on business with Mr. Williams; he was pursued, overtaken, and shot. Mrs. Vaughan's was the next place we visited; and after murdering the family here, I determined on starting for Jerusalem. Our number amounted now to fifty or sixty, all mounted and armed with guns, axes, swords, and clubs. On reaching Mr. James W. Parker's gate, immediately on the road leading to Jerusalem, and about three miles distant, it was proposed to me to call there; but I objected, as I knew he was gone to Jerusalem, and my object was to reach there as soon as possible; but some of the men having relations at Mr. Parker's, it was agreed that they might call and get his people. I remained at the gate on the road, with seven or eight, the others going across the field to the house, about half a mile off. After waiting some time for them, I became impatient, and started to the house for them, and on our return we were met by a party of white men, who had pursued our blood-stained track, and who had fired on those at the gate, and dispersed them, which I knew nothing of, not having been at that time rejoined by any of them. Immediately on discovering the whites, I ordered my men to halt and form, as they appeared to be alarmed. The white men, eighteen in number, approached us in about one hundred yards, when one of them fired, and I discovered about half of them, retreating. I then ordered my men to fire and rush on them ; the few remaining stood their ground until we approached within fifty yards, when they fired and retreated. We pursued and overtook some of them, whom we thought we left dead; after pursuing them about two hundred yards, and rising a little hill, I discovered they were met by another party, and had halted, and were reloading their guns, thinking that those who retreated first, and the party who fired on us at fifty or sixty yards distant, had only fallen back to meet others with ammunition. As I saw them reloading their guns, and more coming up than I saw at first, and several of my bravest men being wounded, the others became panic-struck and scattered over the field; the white men pursued and fired on us several times. Hark had his horse shot under him, and I caught another for him that was running by me; five or six of my men were wounded, but none left on the field. Finding myself defeated here, I instantly determined to go through a private way, and cross the Nottoway River at the Cypress Bridge, three miles below Jerusalem, and attack that place in the rear, as I expected they would look for me on the other road, and I had a great desire to get there to procure arms and ammunition."

Reënforcements came to the whites, and the blacks were overpowered and defeated by the superior numbers of their enemy. In this battle many were slain on both sides. Will, the bloodthirsty and revengeful slave, fell with his broadaxe uplifted, after having laid three of the whites dead at his feet with his own strong arm and his terrible weapon. His last words were, "Bury my axe with me." For he religiously believed that in the next world the blacks would have a contest with the whites, and that he would need his axe. Nat Turner, after fighting to the last with his short sword, escaped with some others to the woods near by, and was not captured for nearly two months. When brought to trial he pleaded "not guilty;" feeling, as he said, that it was always right for one to strike for his own liberty. After going through a mere form of trial, he was convicted and executed at Jerusalem, the county seat for Southampton county, Virginia. Not a limb trembled or a muscle was observed to move. Thus died Nat Turner, at the early age of thirty-one years--a martyr to the freedom of his race, and a victim to his own fanaticism. He meditated upon the wrongs of his oppressed and injured people, till the idea of their deliverance excluded all other ideas from his mind, and he devoted his life to its realization. Every thing appeared to him a vision, and all favorable omens were signs from God. That he was sincere in all that he professed, there is not the slightest doubt. After being defeated he might have escaped to the free states, but the hope of raising a new band kept him from doing so.

He impressed his image upon the minds of those who once beheld him. His looks, his sermons, his acts, and his heroism live in the hearts of his race, on every cotton, sugar, and rice plantation at the south. The present generation of slaves have a superstitious veneration for his name, and believe that in another insurrection Nat Turner will appear and take command. He foretold that at his death the sun would refuse to shine, and that there would be signs of disapprobation given from heaven. And it is true that the sun was darkened, a storm gathered, and more boisterous weather had never appeared in Southampton county than on the day of Nat's execution. The sheriff, warned by the prisoner, refused to cut the cord that held the trap. No black man would touch the rope. A poor old white man, long besotted by drink, was brought forty miles to be the executioner. And even the planters, with all their prejudice and hatred, believed him honest and sincere; for Mr. Gray, who had known Nat from boyhood, and to whom he made his confession, says of him,--

"It has been said that he was ignorant and cowardly, and that his object was to murder and rob, for the purpose of obtaining money to make his escape. It is notorious that he was never known to have a dollar in his life, to swear an oath, or drink a drop of spirits. As to his ignorance, he certainly never had the advantages of education; but he can read and write, and for natural intelligence and quickness of apprehension, is surpassed by few men I have ever seen. As to his being a coward, his reason, as given, for not resisting Mr. Phipps, shows the decision of his character. When he saw Mr. Phipps present his gun, he said he knew it was impossible for him to escape, as the woods were full of men; he therefore thought it was better for him to surrender, and trust to fortune for his escape. He is a complete fanatic, or plays his part most admirably. On other subjects he possesses an uncommon share of intelligence, with a mind capable of attaining any thing, but warped and perverted by the influence of early impressions. He is below the ordinary stature, though strong and active; having the true negro face, every feature of which is strongly marked. I shall not attempt to describe the effect of his narrative, as told and commented on by himself, in the condemned hole of the prison; the calm, deliberate composure with which he spoke of his late deeds and intentions; the expressions of his fiend-like face, when excited by enthusiasm--still bearing the stains of the blood of helpless innocence about him, clothed with rags and covered with chains, yet daring to raise his manacled hands to heaven, with a spirit soaring above the attributes of man; I looked on him, and the blood curdled in my veins."

Well might he feel the blood curdle in his veins, when he remembered that in every southern household there may be a Nat Turner, in whose soul God has lighted a torch of liberty that cannot be extinguished by the hand of man. The slaveholder should understand that he lives upon a volcano, which may burst forth at any moment, and give freedom to his victim.

"Great God, hasten on the glad jubilee,
When my brother in bonds shall arise and be free,
And our blotted escutcheon be washed from its stains,
Now the scorn of the world--four millions in chains!
O, then shall Columbia's proud flag be unfurled,
The glory of freemen, and pride of the world,
While earth's strolling millions point hither in glee,
'To the land of the brave and the home of the free!'"

Fifty-five whites and seventy-three blacks lost their lives in the Southampton rebellion. On the fatal night when Nat and his companions were dealing death to all they found, Captain Harris, a wealthy planter, had his life saved by the devotion and timely warning of his slave Jim, said to have been half-brother to his master. After the revolt had been put down, and parties of whites were out hunting the suspected blacks, Captain Harris, with his faithful slave, went into the woods in search of the negroes. In saving his master's life, Jim felt that he had done his duty, and could not consent to become a betrayer of his race, and, on reaching the woods, he handed his pistol to his master, and said, "I cannot help you hunt down these men; they, like myself, want to be free. Sir, I am tired of the life of a slave; please give me my freedom, or shoot me on the spot." Captain Harris took the weapon and pointed it at the slave. Jim, putting his right hand upon his heart, said, "This is the spot; aim here." The captain fired, and the slave fell dead at his foot.

From this insurrection, and other manifestations of insubordination by the slave population, the southern people, if they are wise, should learn a grave lesson; for the experience of the past might give them some clew to the future.

Thirty years' free discussion has materially changed public opinion in the non-slaveholding states, and a negro insurrection, in the present excited state of the nation, would not receive the condemnation that it did in 1831. The right of man to the enjoyment of freedom is a settled point; and where he is deprived of this, without any criminal act of his own, it is his duty to regain his liberty at every cost.

If the oppressor is struck down in the contest, his fall will be a just one, and all the world will applaud the act.

This is a new era, and we are in the midst of the most important crisis that our country has yet witnessed. And in the crisis the negro is an important item. Every eye is now turned towards the south, looking for another Nat Turner.

## MADISON WASHINGTON.

AMONG the great number of fugitive slaves who arrived in Canada towards the close of the year 1840, was one whose tall figure, firm step, and piercing eye attracted at once the attention of all who beheld him. Nature had treated him as a favorite. His expressive countenance painted and reflected every emotion of his soul. There was a fascination in the gaze of his finely-cut eyes that no one could withstand. Born of African parentage, with no mixture in his blood, he was one of the handsomest of his race. His dignified, calm, and unaffected features announced at a glance that he was one endowed with genius, and created to guide his follow-men. He called himself Madison Washington, and said that his birthplace was in the "Old Dominion." He might have seen twenty-five years; but very few slaves have any correct idea of their age. Madison was not poorly dressed, and had some money at the end of his journey, which showed that he was not from among the worst used slaves of the south. He immediately sought employment at a neighboring farm, where be remained some months. A strong, able-bodied man, and a good worker, and apparently satisfied with his situation, his employer felt that he had a servant who would stay with him long while. The farmer would occasionally raise a conversation, and try to draw from Madison some account of his former life; but in this he failed, for the fugitive was a man of few words, and kept his own secrets. His leisure hours were spent in learning to read and write, and in this he seemed to take the utmost interest. He appeared to take no interest in the sports and amusements that occupied the attention of others. Six months had not passed ere Madison began to show signs of discontent. In vain his employer tried to discover the cause.

"Do I not pay you enough, and treat you in a becoming manner?" asked Mr. Dickson one day when the fugitive seemed in a very desponding mood.

"Yes, sir," replied Madison.

"Then why do you appear so much dissatisfied, of late?"

"Well, sir," said the fugitive, "since you have treated me with such kindness, and seem to take so much interest in me, I will tell you the reason why I have changed, and appear to you to be dissatisfied. I was born in slavery, in the State of Virginia. From my earliest recollections I hated slavery and determined to be free. I have never yet called any man master, though I have been held by three different men who claimed me as their property. The birds in the trees and the wild beasts of the forest made me feel that I, like them, ought to be free. My feelings were all thus centred in the one idea of liberty, of which I thought by day and dreamed by night. I had scarcely reached my twentieth year when I became acquainted with the angelic being who has since become my wife. It was my intention to have escaped with her before we were married, but circumstances prevented.

"I took her to my bosom as my wife, and then resolved to make the attempt. But unfortunately my plans were discovered, and to save myself from being caught and sold off to the far south I escaped to the woods, where I remained during many weary months. As I could not bring my wife away, I would not come without her. Another reason for remaining was, that I hoped to got up an insurrection of the slaves, and thereby be the means of their liberation. In this, too, I failed. At last it was agreed between my wife and me that I should escape to Canada, get employment, save my money, and with it purchase her freedom. With the hope of attaining this end I came into your service. I am now satisfied that, with the wages I can command here, it will take me not less than five years to obtain by my labor the amount sufficient to purchase the liberty of my dear Susan. Five years will be too long for me to wait, for she may die or be sold away ere I can raise the money. This, sir, makes me feel low-spirited, and I have come to the rash determination to return to Virginia for my wife."

The recital of the story had already brought tears to the eyes of the farmer, ere the fugitive had concluded. In vain did Mr. Dickson try to persuade Madison to give up the idea of going back into the very grasp of the tyrant, and risking the loss of his own freedom without securing that of his wife. The heroic man had made up his mind, and nothing could move him. Receiving the amount of wages due him from his employer, Madison turned his face once more towards the south. Supplied with papers purporting to have been made out in Virginia, and certifying to his being a freeman, the fugitive had no difficulty in reaching the neighborhood of his wife. But these "free papers" were only calculated to serve him where he was not known. Madison had also provided himself with files, saws, and other implements with which to cut his way out of any prison into which he might be cast. These instruments were so small as to be easily concealed in the lining of his clothing; and armed with them the fugitive felt sure he should escape again were he ever captured. On his return, Madison met, in the State of Ohio, many of those whom he had seen on his journey to Canada, and all tried to prevail upon him to give up the rash attempt. But to every one he would reply, "Liberty is worth nothing to me while my wife is a slave." When near his former home, and unable to travel in open day without being detected, Madison betook himself to the woods during the day, and travelled by night. At last he arrived at the old farm at night, and hid away in the nearest forest. Here he remained several days, filled with hope and fear, without being able to obtain any information about his wife. One evening, during this suspense, Madison heard the singing of a company of slaves, the sound of which appeared nearer and nearer, until be became convinced that it was a gang going to a corn-shucking, and the fugitive resolved that he would join it, and see if he could get any intelligence of his wife.

In Virginia, as well as in most of the other corn-raising slave states, there is a custom of having what is termed "a corn-shucking," to which slaves from the neighboring plantations, with the consent of their masters, are invited. At the conclusion of the shucking a supper is provided by the owner of the corn; together with the bad whiskey which is freely circulated on such occasions, the slaves are made to feel very happy. Four or five companies of men may be heard in different directions and at the same time approaching the place of rendezvous, slaves joining the gangs along the roads as they pass their masters' farms. Madison came out upon the highway, and as the company came along singing, he fell into the ranks and joined in the song. Through the darkness of the night he was able to keep from being recognized by the remainder of the company,, while he learned from the general conversation the most important news of the day.

Although hungry and thirsty, the fugitive dared not go to the supper table for fear of recognition. However, before he left the company that night, he gained information enough to satisfy him that his wife was still with her old master, and he hoped to see her, if possible, on the following night. The sun had scarcely set the next evening, ere Madison was wending his way out of the forest and going towards the home of his loved one, if the slave can be said to have a home. Susan, the object of his affections, was indeed a woman every way worthy of his love. Madison knew well where to find the room usually occupied by his wife, and to that spot he made his way on arriving at the plantation. But in his zeal and enthusiasm, and his being too confident of success, he committed a blunder which nearly cost him his life. Fearful that if he waited until a late hour Susan would be asleep, and in awakening her she would in her fright alarm the household, Madison ventured to her room too early in the evening, before the whites in the "great house" had retired. Observed by the overseer, a sufficient number of whites were called in, and the fugitive secured ere he could escape with his wife; but the heroic slave did not yield until he with a club had laid three of his assailants upon the ground with his manly blows; and not then until weakened by loss of blood. Madison was at once taken to Richmond, and sold to a slave trader, then making up a gang of slaves for the New Orleans market.

The brig Creole, owned by Johnson & Eperson, of Richmond, and commanded by Captain Enson, lay at the Richmond dock waiting for her cargo, which usually consisted of tobacco, hemp, flax, and slaves. There were two cabins for the slaves, one for the men, the other for the women. The men were generally kept in chains while on the voyage; but the women were usually unchained, and allowed to roam at pleasure in their own cabin. On the 27th of October, 1841, the Creole sailed from Hampton Roads, bound for New Orleans, with her full load of freight, one hundred and thirty-five slaves, and three passengers, besides the crew. Forty of the slaves were owned by Thomas McCargo, nine belonged to Henry Hewell, and the remainder were held by Johnson & Eperson. Howell had once been all overseer for McCargo, and on this occasion was acting as his agent.

Among the slaves owned by Johnson & Eperson was Madison Washington. He was heavily ironed,and chained down to the floor of the cabin occupied by the men, which was in the forward hold. As it was known by Madison's purchasers that he had once escaped and had been in Canada, they kept a watchful eye over him. The two cabins were separated, so that the men and women had no communication whatever during the passage.

Although rather gloomy at times, Madison on this occasion seemed very cheerful, and his owners thought that he had repented of the experience he had undergone as a runaway, and in the future would prove a more easily governed chattel. But from the first hour that he had entered the cabin of the Creole, Madison had been busily engaged in the selection of men who were to act parts in the great drama. He picked out each one as if by intuition. Every thing was done at night and in the dark, as far as the preparation was concerned. The miniature saws and files were faithfully used when the whites were asleep.

In the other cabin, among the slave women, was one whose beauty at once attracted attention. Though not tall, she yet had a majestic figure. Her well-moulded shoulders, prominent bust, black hair which hung in ringlets, mild blue eyes, finely-chiselled month, with a splendid set of teeth, a turned and well-rounded chin, skin marbled with the animation of life, and veined by blood given to her by her master, she stood as the representative of two races. With only one eighth of African, she was what is called at the south an "octoroon." It was said that her grandfather had served his country in the revolutionary war, as well as in both houses of Congress. This was Susan, the wife of Madison. Few slaves, even among the best used house servants, had so good an opportunity to gain general information as she. Accustomed to travel with her mistress, Susan had often been to Richmond, Norfolk, White Sulphur Springs, and other places of resort for the aristocracy of the Old Dominion. Her language was far more correct than most slaves in her position. Susan was as devoted to Madison, as she was beautiful and accomplished.

After the arrest of her husband, and his confinement in Richmond jail, it was suspected that Susan had long been in possession of the knowledge of his whereabouts when in Canada, and knew of his being in the neighborhood; and for this crime it was resolved that she should be sold and sent off to a southern plantation, where all hope of escape would be at an end. Each was not aware that the other was on board the Creole, for Madison and Susan were taken to their respective cabins at different times. On the ninth day out, the Creole encountered a rough sea, and most of the slaves were sick, and therefore were not watched with that vigilance that they had been since she first sailed. This was the time for Madison and his accomplices to work, and nobly did they perform their duty. Night came on; the first watch had just been summoned, the wind blowing high, when Madison succeeded in reaching the quarter deck, followed by eighteen others, all of whom sprang to different parts of the vessel, seizing whatever they could wield as weapons. The crew were nearly all on deck. Captain Enson and Mr. Merritt, the first mate, were standing together, while Howell was seated on the companion smoking a cigar. The appearance of the slaves all at once, and the loud voice and commanding attitude of their leader, so completely surprised the whites, that--

"They spake not a word;
But, like dumb statues, or breathless stones,
Stared at each other, and looked deadly pale."

The officers were all armed; but so swift were the motions of Madison that they had nearly lost command of the vessel before they attempted to use their weapons.

Hewell, the greater part of whose life had been spent on the plantation in the capacity of a negro-driver, and who knew that the defiant looks of these men meant something, was the first to start. Drawing his old horse pistol from under his coat, he fired at one of the blacks and killed him. The next moment Hewell lay dead upon the deck, for Madison had struck him with a capstan bar. The fight now became general, the white passengers, as well as all the crew, taking part. The battle was Madison's element, and he plunged into it without any care for his own preservation or safety. He was an instrument of enthusiasm, whose value and whose place was in his inspiration. "If the fire of heaven was in my hands, I would throw it at these cowardly whites," said he to his companions, before leaving their cabin. But in this he did not mean revenge, only the possession of his freedom and that of his fellow-slaves. Merritt and Gifford, the first and second mates of the vessel, both attacked the heroic slave at the same time. Both were stretched out upon the deck with a single blow each, but were merely wounded; they were disabled, and that was all that Madison cared for for the time being. The sailors ran up the rigging for safety, and a moment more he that had worn the fetters an hour before was master of the brig Creole. His commanding attitude and daring orders, now that he was free and his perfect preparation for the grand alternative of liberty or death which stood before him, are splendid exemplifications of the truly heroic. After his accomplices had covered the slaver's deck, Madison forbade the shedding of more blood, and ordered the sailors to come down, which they did, and with his own hands he dressed their wounds. A guard was placed over all except Merritt, who was retained to navigate the vessel. With a musket doubly charged, and pointed at Merritt's breast, the slave made him swear that he would faithfully take the brig into a British port. All things now secure, and the white men in chains or under guard, Madison ordered that the fetters should be severed from the limbs of those slaves who still wore them. The next morning "Captain Washington" (for such was the name he now bore) ordered the cook to provide the best breakfast that the store room could furnish, intending to surprise his fellow-slaves, and especially the females, whom he had not yet seen. But little did he think that the woman for whom he had risked his liberty and life would meet him at the breakfast table. The meeting of the hero and his beautiful and accomplished wife, the tears of joy shed, and the hurrahs that followed from the men, can better be imagined than described. Madison's cup of joy was filled to the brim. He had not only gained his own liberty and that of one hundred and thirty-four others, but his dear Susan was safe. Only one man, Hewell, had been killed. Captain Enson and others, who were wounded, soon recovered; and were kindly treated by Madison; but they nevertheless proved ungrateful; for on the second night, Captain Enson, Mr. Gifford, and Merritt took advantage of the absence of Madison from the deck, and attempted to retake the vessel. The slaves, exasperated at this treachery, fell upon the whites with deadly weapons. The captain and his men fled to the cabin, pursued by the blacks. Nothing but the heroism of the negro leader saved the lives of the white men on this occasion, for as the slaves were rushing into the cabin, Madison threw himself between them and their victims, exclaiming, "Stop! no more blood. My life, that was perilled for your liberty, I will lay down for the protection of these men. They have proved themselves unworthy of life, which we granted them; still let us be magnanimous." By the kind heart and noble bearing of Madison, the vile slave-traders were again permitted to go unwhipped of justice. This act of humanity raised the uncouth son of Africa far above his Anglo-Saxon oppressors.

The next morning the Creole landed at Nassau, New Providence, where the noble and heroic slaves were warmly greeted by the inhabitants, who at once offered protection, and extended their hospitality to them. Not many months since, an American ship went ashore at Nassau, and among the first to render assistance to the crew was Madison Washington.

# HENRY BIBB.

HENRY BIBB, like most fugitive slaves, did not know who his father was; that his mother was a slave was sufficient to decide his lot, and to send him, under fear of the lash, while yet a mere infant, to labor on his master's farm: when sufficiently old to be of much use to any one, he was hired out to one person and another for the space of eight or ten years, the proceeds of his labor going, we are told, to defray the expense of educating his owner's daughters. The year of Henry Bibb's birth was a memorable one-- 1815; little, however, knew he of European struggles; he had a great battle of his own to fight against tremendous odds, and he seems to have fought it bravely. He formed the determination to be free at a very early age, and nothing could shake it; starvation, imprisonment, scourging, lacerating, punishments of every kind, and of every degree of severity short of actual death, were tried in vain; they could not subdue his indomitable spirit.

His first attempt to escape was made when he was about ten years of age, and from that time to 1840 his life was a constant series of flights and recaptures, the narrative of which makes one thrill and shudder at the sufferings endured and the barbarities inflicted. Securing his freedom by his own good legs, Henry Bibb at once began seeking an education; and in this he succeeded far beyond many white men who have had all the avenues to learning open to them. In personal appearance he was tall and slim, a pleasing countenance, half white, hair brown, eyes gray, and possessed a musical voice, and a wonderful power of delivery. No one who heard Mr. Bibb, in the years 1847, '8, and '9, can forget the deep impression that he left behind him. His natural eloquence and his songs enchained an audience as long as the speaker wanted them. In 1849, we believe, he went to Canada, and started a weekly paper called The Voice of the Fugitives, at Windsor. His journal was well conducted, and was long regarded as indispensable in every fugitive's house. His first wife being left in slavery, and no hope of her escaping, Mr. Bibb married for his second wife the well-educated and highly-cultivated Mary E. Miles, of Boston. After being in Canada a while, the two opened a school for their escaped brothers and sisters, which proved a lasting benefit to that much-injured class. His efforts to purchase a tract of land, and to deal it out in lots to the fugitives at a reasonable price, was only one of the many kind acts of this good man. There are few characters more worthy of the student's study and imitation than that of Henry Bibb. From all ignorant slave, he became all educated free man, by his own powers, and left a name that will not soon fade away.

In one of Cassimir de la Vigne's dramas, we met with an expression which struck us forcibly. It was said of Don John, who was ignorant of his birth, that perhaps he was a nobody; to which he replied, "That a man of good character and honorable conduct could never be a nobody." We consider this an admirable reply, and have endeavored to prove this truth by the foregoing example. If it is gratifying and noble to boar with honor the name of one's father, it is surely more noble to make a name for one's self; and our heart tells us that among our young readers there is more than one who will exclaim with ardor, and with a firm resolution to fulfil his promise, I, too, shall make a name.

## PLACIDO.

IN the year 1830, there was a young man in Havana, son of a woman who had been brought, when a child, from the coast of Africa, and sold as a slave. Being with a comparatively kind master, he soon found opportunity to begin developing the genius which at a later period showed itself. The young slave was called Placido. He took an especial interest in poetry, and often wrote poems that were set to music and sung in the drawing rooms of the most refined companies which assembled in the city. His young master paying his addresses to a rich heiress, the slave was requested to write a poem embodying the master's passion for the young lady. Placido acquitted himself to the entire satisfaction of the lover, who copied the epistle in his own hand, and sent it on its mission. The slave's compositions were so much admired that they found their way into the newspaper; but no one knew the negro as the author. In 1838, these poems, together with a number which had never appeared in print, were intrusted to a white man, who sent them to England, where they were published and much praised for the talent and scholarly attainment which they developed. A number of young whites, who were well acquainted with Placido and his genius, resolved to purchase him and present him his freedom, which they did in the year 1842. But a new field had opened itself to the freed black, and he began to tread in its paths. Freedom for himself was only the beginning; he sighed to make others free. The imaginative brain of the poet produced verses which the slaves sung in their own rude way, and which kindled in their hearts a more intense desire for liberty. Placido planned an insurrection of the slaves, in which he was to be their leader and deliverer; but the scheme failed. After a hasty trial, he was convicted and sentenced to death. The fatal day came; he walked to the place of execution with as much calmness as if it had been to an ordinary resort of pleasure. His manly and heroic bearing excited the sympathy and admiration of all who saw him. As he arrived at the fatal spot he began reciting the following hymn, which he had written in his cell the previous night:--

## TO GOD--A PRAYER.

"Almighty God! whose goodness knows no bound,
To thee I flee in my severe distress;
O let thy potent arm my wrongs redress,
And rend the odious veil by slander wound
About my brow. The base world's arm confound,
Who on my front would now the seal of shame impress.

God of my sires, to whom all kings must yield,
Be thou alone my shield; protect me now:
All power is His, to whom the sea doth owe
His countless stores; who clothed with light heaven's field,
And made the sun, and air, and polar seas congealed;
All plants with life endowed, and made the rivers flow.

All power is thine: 'twas thy creative might
This goodly frame of things from chaos brought,
Which unsustained by thee would still be nought,
As erst it lay deep in the womb of night,
Ere thy dread word first called it into light;
Obedient to thy call, it lived, and moved, and thought.

Thou know'st my heart, O God, supremely wise;
Thine eye, all-seeing, cannot be deceived;
By thee mine inmost soul is clear perceived,
As objects gross are through transparent skies
By mortal ken. Thy mercy exercise,
Lest slander foul exult o'er innocence aggrieved.

But if 'tis fixed, by thy decree divine,
That I must bear the pain of guilt and shame,
And that my foes this cold and senseless frame
Shall rudely treat with scorn and shouts malign,
Give thou the word, and I my breath resign,
Obedient to thy will. Blest be thy holy name!"

When all preparation for the execution had been finished, Placido asked the privilege of giving the signal, and it was granted. With his face wearing an expression of almost superhuman courage, he said in Spanish, "Adieu, O world; there is no justice or pity for me here. Soldiers, fire!" Five balls entered his body, but did not deprive him of life. Still unsubdued, he again spoke, and placing his hand on his breast, said, "Fire here." Two balls from the reserve entered his heart, and he fell dead.

Thus died Placido, the slave's poet of freedom. His songs are still sung in the bondman's hut, and his name is a household word to all. As the Marseillaise was sung by the revolutionists of France, and inspired the people with a hatred to oppressors, so will the slaves of Cuba, at a future day, sing the songs of their poet-martyr, and their cry will be, "Placido and Liberty."

## JEREMIAH B. SANDERSON.

NEW BEDFORD has produced a number of highly-intelligent men of the "doomed race;" men who, by their own efforts, have attained positions, intellectually, which, if they had been of the more favored class, would have introduced them into the halls of Congress. One of these is J. B. Sanderson. An industrious student, and an ardent lover of literature, he has read more than almost any one of his years within our circle of acquaintance. History, theology, and the classics, he is master of. We first met him while he was on a tour through the west, as a lecturer on slavery, and the impression then made on our mind became still stronger as we knew more of him. Although not at the time an ordained minister Mr. Sanderson, in 1848, preached for one of the religious societies of New Bedford, on Sunday, and attended to his vocation (hair dresser) during the week. Some of the best educated of the whites were always in attendance on these occasions. His sermons were generally beyond the comprehension of his bearers, except those well read. Emerson, Carlyle, and Theodore Parker, were represented in his discourses, which were always replete with historical incidents. Mr. Sanderson has been several years in California, where he now preaches to an intelligent congregation and is considered one of the ablest religious teachers in the Pacific state.

> "Honor and fame from no condition rise:
> Act well your part-- there all the honor lies."

> "Who does the best his circumstance allows,
> Does well, acts nobly: angels could no more."

In stature Mr. Sanderson is somewhat above the medium height, finely formed, well-developed head, and a pleasing face; an excellent voice, which he knows how to use. His gestures are correct without being studied, and his sentences always tell upon his audience. Few speakers are more happy in their delivery than he. In one of those outbursts of true eloquence for which he is so noted, we still remember the impression made upon his hearers, when, on one occasion, he exclaimed, "Neither men nor governments have a right to sell those of their species; men and their liberty are neither purchasable nor salable. This is the law of nature, which is obligatory on all men, at all times, and in all places."

All accounts from California speak of J. B. Sanderson as doing more for the enfranchisement and elevation of his race than any one who has gone from the Atlantic states.

## TOUSSAINT L'OUVERTURE.

AT the commencement of the French revolution, in 1789, there were nine hundred thousand inhabitants on the Island of St. Domingo. Of these, seven hundred thousand were Africans, sixty thousand mixed blood, and the remainder were whites and Caribbeans. Like the involuntary servitude in our own Southern States, slavery in St. Domingo kept morality at a low stand. Owing to the amalgamation between masters and slaves, there arose the mulatto population, which eventually proved to be the worst enemies of their fathers.

Many of the planters sent their mulatto sons to France to be educated. When these young men returned to the island, they were greatly dissatisfied at the proscription which met them wherever they appeared. White enough to make them hopeful and aspiring, many of the mulattoes possessed wealth enough to make them influential. Aware, by their education, of the principles of freedom that were being advocated in Europe and the United States, they were ever on the watch to seize opportunities to better their social and political condition. In the French part of the island alone, twenty thousand whites lived in the midst of thirty thousand free mulattoes and five hundred thousand slaves. In the Spanish portion, the odds were still greater in favor of the slaves. Thus the advantage of numbers and physical strength was on the side of the oppressed. Right is the most dangerous of weapons--woe to him who leaves it to his enemies!

The efforts of Wilberforce, Sharp, Buxton, and Clarkson to abolish the African slave trade, and their advocacy of the equality of the races, were well understood by the men of color. They had also learned their own strength in the island, and that they had the sympathy of all Europe with them. The news of the oath of the Tennis Court and the taking of the Bastile at Paris was received with the wildest enthusiasm by the people of St. Domingo.

The announcement of these events was hailed with delight by both the white planters and the mulattoes; the former, because they hoped that a revolution in the mother country would secure to them the independence of the colony; the latter, because they viewed it as a movement that would give them equal rights with the whites; and even the slaves regarded it as a precursor to their own emancipation. But the excitement which the outbreak at Paris had created amongst the free men of color and the slaves, at once convinced the planters that a separation from France would be the death-knell of slavery in St. Domingo.

Although emancipated by law from the dominion of individuals, the mulattoes had no rights: shut out from society by their color, deprived of religious and political privileges, they felt their degradation even more keenly than the bond slaves. The mulatto son was not allowed to dine at his father's table, kneel with him in his devotions, bear his name, inherit his property, nor even to lie in his father's graveyard. Laboring as they were under the sense of their personal social wrongs, the mulattoes tolerated, if they did not encourage, low and vindictive passions. They were haughty and disdainful to the blacks, whom they scorned, and jealous and turbulent to the whites, whom they hated and feared.

The mulattoes at once despatched one of their number to Paris, to lay before the Constitutional Assembly their claim to equal rights with the whites. Vincent Ogé, their deputy, was well received at Paris by Lafayette, Brissot, Barnave, and Gregoire, and was admitted to a seat in the Assembly, where he eloquently portrayed the wrongs of his race. In urging his claims, he said, if equality was withheld from the mulattoes, they would appeal to force. This was seconded by Lafayette and Barnave, who said, "Perish the colonies rather than a principle."

The Assembly passed a decree granting the demands of the men of color, and Ogé was made bearer of the news to his brethren. The planters armed themselves, met the young deputy on his return to the island, and a battle ensued. The free colored men rallied around Ogé, but they were defeated and taken, with their brave leader, were first tortured, and then broken alive on the wheel.

The prospect of freedom was put down for the time, but the blood of Ogé and his companions bubbled silently in the hearts of the African race; they swore to avenge them.

The announcement of the death of Ogé in the halls of the Assembly at Paris created considerable excitement, and became the topic of conversation in the clubs and on the Boulevards. Gregoire defended the course of the colored men, and said, "If Liberty was right in France, it was right in St. Domingo." He well knew that the crime for which Ogé had suffered in the West Indies, had constituted the glory of Mirabeau and Lafayette at Paris, and Washington and Hancock in the United States. The planters in the island trembled at their own oppressive acts, and terror urged them on to greater violence. The blood of Ogé and his accomplices had sown every where despair and conspiracy. The French sent an army to St. Domingo to enforce the laws.

The planters repelled with force the troops sent out by France, denying its prerogatives and refusing the civic oath. In the midst of these thickening troubles, the planters who resided in France were invited to return and assist in vindicating the civil independence of the island. Then was it that the mulattoes earnestly appealed to the slaves, and the result was appalling. The slaves awoke as from an ominous dream, and demanded their rights with sword in hand. Gaining immediate success, and finding that their liberty would not be granted by the planters, they rapidly increased in numbers; and in less than a week from its commencement, the storm had swept over the whole plain of the north, from east to west, and from the mountains to the sea. The splendid villas and rich factories yielded to the furies of the devouring flames; so that the mountains, covered with smoke and burning cinders, borne upwards by the wind, looked like volcanoes; and the atmosphere, as if on fire, resembled a furnace.

Such were the outraged feelings of a people whose ancestors had been ruthlessly torn from their native land, and sold in the shambles of St. Domingo. To terrify the blacks and convince them that they could could never be free, the planters were murdering them on every hand by thousands.

The struggle in St. Domingo was watched with intense interest by the friends of the blacks, both in Paris and in London, and all appeared to look with hope to the rising up of a black chief, who should prove himself adequate to the emergency. Nor did they look in vain. In the midst of the disorders that threatened on all sides, the negro chief made his appearance in the person of a slave, named Toussaint. This man was the grandson of the King of Ardra, one of the most powerful and wealthy monarchs on the west coast of Africa. By his own energy and perseverance, Toussaint had learned to read and write, and was held in high consideration by the surrounding planters as well as their slaves.

His private virtues were many, and he had a deep and pervading sense of religion, and in the camp carried it even as far as Oliver Cromwell. Toussaint was born on the island, and was fifty years of age when called into the field. One of his chief characteristics was his humanity.

Before taking any part in the revolution, he aided his master's family to escape from the impending danger. After seeing them beyond the reach of the revolutionary movement, he entered the army as an inferior officer, but was soon made aid-de-camp to General Bissou. Disorder and bloodshed reigned throughout the island, and every day brought fresh intelligence of depredations committed by whites, mulattoes, and blacks.

Such was the condition of affairs when a decree was passed by the Colonial Assembly giving equal rights to the mulattoes, and asking their aid in restoring order and reducing the slaves again to their chains. Overcome by this decree, and having gained all they wished, the free colored men joined the planters in a murderous crusade against the slaves. This union of the whites and mulattoes to prevent the bondman getting his freedom, created an ill feeling between the two proscribed classes which seventy years have not been able to efface. The French government sent a second army to St. Domingo, to enforce the laws giving freedom to the slaves; and Toussaint joined it on its arrival in the island, and fought bravely against the planters.

While the people of St. Domingo were thus fighting amongst themselves, the revolutionary movement in France had fallen into the hands of Robespierre and Danton, and the guillotine was beheading its thousands daily. When the news of the death of Louis XVI. reached St. Domigo, Toussaint and his companions left the French, and joined the Spanish army in the eastern part of the island, and fought for the kin of Spain. Here Toussaint was made brigadier general, and appeared in the field as the most determined foe of the French planters.

The two armies met; a battle was fought in the streets, and many thousands were slain on both sides; the planters, however, were defeated. During the conflict the city was set on fire, and on every side presented shocking evidence of slaughter, conflagration, and pillage. The strifes of political and religious partisanship, which had raged in the clubs and streets of Paris, were transplanted to St. Domingo, where they raged with all the heat of a tropical clime and the animosities of a civil war. Truly did the flames of the French revolution at Paris, and the ignorance and self-will of the planters, set the island of St. Domingo on fire. The commissioners, with their retinue, retired from the burning city into the neighboring highlands, where a camp was formed to protect the ruined town from the opposing party. Having no confidence in the planters, and fearing a reaction, the commissioners proclaimed a general emancipation to the slave population, and invited the blacks who had joined the Spaniards to return. Toussaint and his followers accepted the invitation, returned, and were enrolled in the army under the commissioners. Fresh troops arrived from France, who were no sooner in the island than they separated--some siding with the planters, and others with the commissioners. The white republicans of the mother country arrayed themselves against the white republicans of St. Domingo, whom they were sent out to assist; the blacks and the mulattoes were at war with each other; old and young, of both sexes and of all colors, were put to the sword, while the fury of the flames swept from plantation to plantation and from town to town.

During these sad commotions, Toussaint, by his superior knowledge of the character of his race, his humanity, generosity, and courage, had gained the confidence of all whom he had under his command. The rapidity with which he travelled from post to post astonished every one. By his genius and surpassing activity, Toussaint levied fresh forces, raised the reputation of the army, and drove the English and Spanish from the island.

With the termination of this struggle every vestige of slavery and all obstacles to freedom disappeared. Toussaint exerted every nerve to make Hayti what it had formerly been. He did every thing in his power to promote agriculture; and in this he succeeded beyond the most sanguine expectations of the friends of freedom, both in England and France. Even the planters who had remained on the island acknowledged the prosperity of Hayti under the governorship of the man whose best days had been spent in slavery.

The peace of Amiens left Bonaparte without a rival on the continent, and with a large and experienced army, which he feared to keep idle; and he determined to send a part of it to St. Domingo.

The army for the expedition to St. Domingo was fitted out, and no pains or expense spared to make it an imposing one. Fifty-six ships of war, with twenty-five thousand men, left France for Hayti. It was,indeed, the most valiant fleet that had ever sailed from the French dominions. The Alps, the Nile, the Rhine, and all Italy, had resounded with the exploits of the men who were now leaving their country for the purpose of placing the chains again on the limbs of the heroic people of St. Domingo. There were men in that army that had followed Bonaparte from the siege of Toulon to the battle under the shades of the pyramids of Egypt-- men who had grown gray in the camp.

News of the intended invasion reached St. Domingo some days before the squadron had sailed from Brest; and therefore the blacks had time to prepare to meet their enemies. Toussaint had concentrated his forces at such points as he expected would be first attacked. Christophe was sent to defend Cape City, and Port-au-Prince was left in the hands of Dessalines.

With no navy, and but little means of defence, the Haytians determined to destroy their towns rather than they should fall into the hands of the enemy. Late in the evening the French ships were seen to change their position, and Christophe, satisfied that they were about to effect a landing, set fire to his own house, which was the signal for the burning of the town. The French general wept as he beheld the ocean of flames rising from the tops of the houses in the finest city in St. Domingo. Another part of the fleet landed in Samana, where Toussaint, with an experienced wing of the army, was ready to meet them. On seeing the ships enter the harbor, the heroic chief said, "Here come the enslavers of our race. All France is coming to St. Domingo, to try again to put the fetters upon our limbs; but not France, with all her troops of the Rhine, the Alps, the Nile, the Tiber, nor all Europe to help her, can extinguish the soul of Africa. That soul, when once the soul of a man, and no longer that of a slave, can overthrow the pyramids and the Alps themselves, sooner than again be crushed down into slavery." The French, however, effected a landing, but they found nothing but smouldering ruins, where once stood splendid cities. Toussaint and his generals at once abandoned the towns, and betook themselves to the mountains, those citadels of freedom in St. Domingo, where the blacks have always proved too much for the whites.

Toussaint put forth a proclamation to the colored people, in which he said, "You are now to meet and fight enemies who have neither faith, law, nor religion. Lot us resolve that these French troops shall never leave our shores alive." The war commenced, and the blacks were victorious in nearly all the battles. Where the French gained a victory, they put their prisoners to the most excruciating tortures; in many instances burning them in pits, and throwing them into boiling caldrons. This example of cruelty set by the whites was followed by the blacks. Then it was that Dessalines, the ferocious chief, satisfied his long pent-up revenge against the white planters and French soldiers that he made prisoners. The French general saw that he could gain nothing from the blacks on the field of battle, and he determined upon a stratagem, in which he succeeded too well.

A correspondence was opened with Toussaint, in which the captain-general promised to acknowledge the liberty of the blacks and the equality of all, if he would yield. Overcome by the persuasions of his generals and the blacks who surrounded him, and who were sick and tired of the shedding of blood, Toussaint gave in his adhesion to the French authorities. This was the great error of his life.

Vincent, in his "Reflections on the Present State of the Colony of St. Domingo," says, "Toussaint, at the head of his army, is the most active and indefatigable man of whom we can form an idea; we may say, with truth, that he is found wherever instructions or danger render his presence necessary. The particular care which he employs in his march, of always deceiving the men of whom he has need, and who think they enjoy a confidence he gives to none, has such an effect that he is daily expected in all the chief places of the colony. His great sobriety, the faculty, which none but he possesses, of never reposing, the facility with which he resumes the affairs of the cabinet after the most tiresome excursions, of answering daily a hundred letters, and of habitually tiring five secretaries, render him so superior to all those around him, that their respect and submission are in most individuals carried even to fanaticism. It is certain that no man, in the present times, has possessed such an influence over a mass of people as General Toussaint possesses over his brethren in St. Domingo."

The above is the opinion of an enemy--one who regarded the negro chief as a dangerous man to his interest.

Invited by the captain-general of the island to attend a council, the black hero was treacherously seized and sent on board the ship of war Hero, which set sail at once for France. On the arrival of the illustrious prisoner at Brest, he was taken in a close carriage and transferred to the castle of Joux, in the Lower Pyrenees. The gelid atmosphere of the mountain region, the cold, damp dungeon in which he was placed, with the water dripping upon the floor day and night, did not hasten the death of Toussaint fast enough. By Napoleon's directions the prisoner's servant was taken from him, sufficient clothing and bedding to keep him warm were denied, his food curtailed, and his keeper, after an absence of four days, returned and found the hero of St. Domingo dead in his cell. Thus terminated the career of a self-made man.

Toussaint was of prepossessing appearance, of middle stature, and possessed an iron frame. His dignified, calm, and unaffected features, and broad and well-developed forehead, would cause him to be selected, in any company of men, as one born for a leader. Endowed by nature with high qualities of mind, he owed his elevation to his own energies and his devotion to the welfare and freedom of his race. His habits were thoughtful; and like most men of energetic temperaments, he crowded much into what he said. So profound and original were his opinions, that they have been successively drawn upon by all the chiefs of St. Domingo since his era, and still without loss of adaptation to the circumstances of the country. The policy of his successors has been but a repetition of his plans, and his maxims are still the guidance of the rulers of Hayti. His thoughts were copious and full of vigor, and what he could express well in his native patois he found tame and unsatisfactory in the French language, which he was obliged to employ in the details of his official business. He would never sign what he did not fully understand, obliging two or three secretaries to re-word the document, until they had succeeded in furnishing the particular phrase expressive of his meaning. While at the height of his power, and when all around him were furnished with every comfort, and his officers living in splendor, Toussaint himself lived with an austere sobriety which bordered on abstemiousness. He was entirely master of his own passions and appetites. It was his custom to set off in his carriage with the professed object of going to some particular point of the island, and when he had passed over several miles of the journey, to quit the carriage, which continued its route under the same escort of guards, while Toussaint, mounted on horseback and followed by his officers, made rapid excursions across the country, to places where he was least expected. It was upon one of these occasions that he owed his life to his singular mode of travelling. He had just left his carriage when an ambuscade of mulattoes, concealed in the thickets of Boucassin, fired upon the guard, and several balls pierced the carriage, and one of them killed an old domestic who occupied the seat of his master. No person knew better than he the art of governing the people under his jurisdiction. The greater part of the population loved him to idolatry. Veneration for Toussaint was not confined to the boundaries of St. Domingo; it ran through Europe; and in France his name was frequently pronounced in the senate with the eulogy of polished eloquence. No one can look back upon his career without feeling that Toussaint was a remarkable man. Without being bred to the science of arms, he became a valiant soldier, and baffled the skill of the most experienced generals that had followed Napoleon.

Without military knowledge he fought like one born in the camp. Without means he carried on the war. He beat his enemies in battle, and turned their own weapons against them. He laid the foundation for the emancipation of his race and the independence of the island. From ignorance he became educated by his own exertions. From a slave he rose to be a soldier, a general, and a governor, and might have been king of St. Domingo. He possessed splendid traits of genius, which was developed in the private circle, in the council chamber, and on the field of battle. His very name became a tower of strength to his friends and a terror to his foes. Toussaint's career as a Christian, a statesman, and a general, will lose nothing by a comparison with that of Washington. Each was the leader of an oppressed and outraged people, each had a powerful enemy to contend with , and each succeeded in founding a government in the new world. Toussaint's government made liberty its watchword, incorporated it in its constitution, abolished the slave trade, and made freedom universal amongst the people. Washington's government incorporated slavery and the slave trade, and enacted laws by which chains were fastened upon the limbs of millions of people. Toussaint liberated his countrymen; Washington enslaved a portion of his. When impartial history shall do justice to the St. Domingo revolution, the name of Toussaint L'Ouverture will be placed high upon the roll of fame.

## CRISPUS ATTUCKS.

THE principle that taxation and representation were inseparable was in accordance with the theory, the genius, and the precedents of British legislation; and this principle was now, for the first time, intentionally invaded. The American colonies were not represented in Parliament; yet an act was passed by that body, the tendency of which was to invalidate all right and title to their property. This was the "Stamp Act," of March 28, 1765, which ordained that no sale, bond, note of hand, or other instrument of writing should be valid unless executed on paper bearing the stamp prescribed by the home government. The intelligence of the passage of the stamp act at once roused the indignation of the liberty-loving portion of the people of the colonies, and meetings were held at various points to protest against this high-handed measure. Massachusetts was the first to take a stand in opposition to the mother country. The merchants and traders of Boston, New York, and Philadelphia entered into non-importation agreements, with a view of obtaining a repeal of the obnoxious law. Under the pressure of public sentiment, the stamp act officers gave in their resignations. The eloquence of William Pitt and the sagacity of Lord Camden brought about a repeal of the stamp act in the British Parliament. A new ministry, in 1767, succeeded in getting through the House of Commons a bill to tax the tea imported into the American colonies, and it received the royal assent. Massachusetts again took the lead in opposing the execution of this last act, and Boston began planning to take the most conspicuous part in the great drama. The agitation in the colonies provoked the home government, and power was given to the governor of Massachusetts to take notice of all persons who might offer any treasonable objections to these oppressive enactments, that the same might be sent home to England to be tried there. Lord North was now at the head of affairs, and no leniency was to be shown to the colonies. The concentration of British troops in large numbers at Boston convinced the people that their liberties were at stake, and they began to rally. A crowded and enthusiastic meeting, held in Boston in the latter part of the year 1769, was addressed by the ablest talent that the progressive element could produce. Standing in the back part of the hall, eagerly listening to the speakers, was a dark mulatto man, very tall, rather good looking, and apparently about fifty years of age. This was Crispus Attucks. Though taking no part in the meeting, he was nevertheless destined to be conspicuous in the first struggle in throwing off the British yoke. Twenty years previous to this, Attucks was the slave of William Brouno, Esq., of Framingham, Mass.; but his was a heart beating for freedom, and not to be kept in the chains of mental or bodily servitude.

From the Boston Gazette of Tuesday, November 20, 1750, now in the possession of William C. Nell, Esq., I copy the following advertisement:--

"Ran away from his master William Brouno Framingham, on the 30th of Sept., last, a Molatto Fellow, about 27 years of Age named Crispus, well set, six feet 2 inches high, short curl'd Hair, knees nearer together than common; had on a light coloured Bearskin Coat, brown Fustian jacket, new Buckskin Breeches, blew yarn Stockins and Checkered Shirt. Whoever shall take up said Run-away, and convey him to his above said Master at Framingham, shall have Ten Pounds, Old Tenor Reward and all necessary Charges paid."

The above is a verbatim et literatim advertisement for a runaway slave one hundred and twelve years ago. Whether Mr. Brouno succeeded in recapturing Crispus or not, we are left in the dark.

Ill-feeling between the mother country and her colonial subjects had been gaining ground, while British troops were concentrating at Boston. On the 5th of March, 1770, the people were seen early congregating at the corners of the principal streets, at Dock Square, arid near the custom house. Captain Preston, with a body of redcoats, started out for the purpose of keeping order in the disaffected town, and was hissed at by the crowds in nearly every place where he appeared. The day passed off without any outward manifestation of disturbance, but all seemed to feel that something would take place after nightfall. The doubling of the guard in and about the custom house showed that the authorities felt an insecurity that they did not care to express. The lamps in Dock Square threw their light in the angry faces of a large crowd who appeared to be waiting for the crisis, in whatever form it should come. A part of Captain Preston's company was making its way from the custom house, when they were met by the crowd from Dock Square, headed by the black man Attucks, who was urging them to meet the red-coats, and drive them from the streets. "These rebels have no business here," said he; "let's drive them away." The people became enthusiastic, their brave leader grew more daring in his language and attitude, while the soldiers under Captain Preston appeared to give way. "Come on! don't be afraid!" cried Attucks. "They dare not shoot; and if they dare, let them do it." Stones and sticks, with which the populace was armed, were freely used, to the great discomfiture of the English soldiers. "Don't hesitate! come on! We'll drive these rebels out of Boston," were the last words heard from the lips of the colored man, for the sharp crack of muskets silenced his voice, and he fell weltering in his blood. Two balls had pierced his sable breast. Thus died Crispus Attucks, the first martyr to American liberty, and the inaugurator of the revolution that was destined to take from the crown of George the Third its brightest star. An immense concourse of citizens followed the remains of the hero to its last resting place, and his name was honorably mentioned in the best circles. The last words, the daring, and the death of Attucks gave spirit and enthusiasm to the revolution, and his heroism was imitated by both whites arid blacks. His name was a rallying cry for the brave colored men who fought at the battle of Bunker's Hill. In the gallant defence of Redbank, where four hundred blacks met arid defeated fifteen hundred Hessians headed by Count Donop, the thought of Attucks filled them with ardor. When Colonel Greene fell at Groton, surrounded by his black troops who perished with him, they went into the battle feeling proud of the opportunity of imitating the first martyr of the American revolution.

No monument has yet been erected to him. An effort was made in the legislature of Massachusetts a few years since, but without success. Five generations of accumulated prejudice against the negro had excluded from the American mind all inclination to do justice to one of her bravest sons. When negro slavery shall be abolished in our land, then we may hope to see a monument raised to commemorate the heroism of Crispus Attucks.

# DESSALINES.

JEAN JACQUES DESSALINES was a native of Africa. Brought to St. Domingo at the age of sixteen, he was sold to a black man named Dessalines, from whom he took his own. His master was a tiler or house-shingler, and the slave learned that trade, at which he worked until the breaking out of the revolution of 1789, when he entered the army as a common soldier, under Toussaint. By his activity and singular fierceness on the field of battle, Dessalines attracted the attention of his general, who placed him among his guides and personal attendants; and he was subsequently rapidly advanced through several intermediate grades to the dignity of being the third in command. He was entirely ignorant of learning, as the utmost extent that he ever acquired was to sign his name. Dessalines was short in stature, but stout and muscular. His complexion was a dingy black; his eyes were prominent and scowling, and the lines of his features expressed the untamed ferocity of his character. He had a haughty and disdainful look. Hunger, thirst, fatigue, and loss of sleep he seemed made to endure as if by peculiarity of constitution. He bore upon his arms and breast the marks of his tribe. Inured by exposure and toil to a hard life, his frame possessed a wonderful power of endurance. He was a bold and turbulent spirit, whose barbarous eloquence lay in expressive signs rather than in words. What is most strange in the history of Dessalines is, that he was a savage, a slave, a soldier, a general, and died, when an emperor, under the dagger of a Brutus.

A more courageous man than he never lived. Fearing that his men, during the attack upon the fort at Crete-a-Pierrot, would surrender it, he seized a torch, held it to the door of the magazine, and threatened to blow up the fort, and himself with it, if they did not defend it. Nearly all historians have set him down as a bloodthirsty monster, who delighted in the sufferings of his fellow-creatures. They do not rightly consider the circumstances that surrounded him, and the foe that he had to deal with.

Rochambeau, the commanding general, from the landing of Napoleon's expedition to the entire expulsion of the French, was a hard-hearted slaveholder, many of whose years had been spent in St. Domingo, and who, from the moment that he landed with his forces, treated the colored men as the worst of barbarians and wild beasts. He imported bloodhounds from Cuba to hunt them down in the mountains. When caught, he had them thrown into burning pits and boiling caldrons. When he took prisoners, he put them to the most excruciating tortures and the most horrible deaths. His ferocious and sanguinary spirit was too much for the kind heart of Toussaint, or the gentlemanly bearing of Christophe. His only match was Dessalines.

In a battle near Cape François, Rochambeau took five hundred black prisoners, and put them all to death the same day. Dessalines, hearing of this, brought five hundred white prisoners in sight of the French, and hung them up, so that the cruel monster could see the result of his own barbarous example.

Although Toussaint was away from the island, the war seemed to rage with greater fury than at any former period. The blacks grew wild as they looked upon the flames; they became conscious of their power and success; gaining confidence and increasing their numbers, all the pent-up feelings and hatred of years burst forth, and they pushed forward upon defenceless men, women, and children. The proud, haughty, and self-sufficient planter, who had been permitted, under the mild rule of Toussaint, to return and establish himself on his former estate, had to give way again to the terrible realities which came upon him.

The fertile plains that were in the highest state of cultivation, the lively green of the sugar-cane that filled the landscape through boundless fields, and the plantations of indigo and coffee, with all their beautiful hues of vegetation, were destroyed by the flames and smoke which spread every where. Dessalines was the commander-in-chief in fact, though he shared the name with Christophe and Clervaux. Forty thousand French troops had already perished by yellow fever and the sword. Leclerc, the captain-general of the island, lay sick, the hospitals were filled, and the blacks had possession of nearly all the towns.

Twenty thousand fresh troops arrived from France, but they were not destined to see Leclerc, for the yellow fever had taken him off. In the mountains were many barbarous and wild blacks, who had escaped from slavery soon after being brought from the coast of Africa. One of these bands of savages was commanded by Lamour de Rance, an adroit, stern, savage man, half naked, with epaulets tied to his bare shoulders for his only token of authority. This man had been brought from the coast of Africa, and sold as a slave in Port au Prince. On being ordered one day to saddle his master's horse, he did so, then mounted the animal, fled to the mountains, and ever after made those fearful regions his home. Lamour passed from mountain to mountain with something of the ease of the birds of his own native land. Toussaint, Christophe, and Dessalines, had each in their turn pursued him, but in vain. His mode of fighting was in keeping with his dress. This savage united with others like himself, and became complete master of the wilds of St. Domingo. They came forth from their mountain homes, and made war on the whites wherever they found them. Rochambeau, surrounded on all sides, drew his army together for defence rather than aggression. Reduced to the last extremity by starvation, the French general sued for peace, and promised that he would immediately leave the island. It was accepted by the blacks, and Rochambeau prepared to return to France. The French embarked in their vessels of war, and the standard of the blacks once more waved over Cape City, the capital of St. Domingo. As the French sailed from the island, they saw the tops of the mountains lighted up. It was not a blaze kindled for war, but for freedom. Every heart beat for liberty, and every voice shouted for joy. From the ocean to the mountains, and from town to town, the cry was, Freedom! Freedom! Thus ended Napoleon's expedition to St. Domingo. In less than two years the French lost more than fifty thousand persons. After the retirement of the whites, the men of color put forth a Declaration of Independence, in which they said, "We have sworn to show no mercy to those who may dare to speak to us of slavery."

The bravery and military skill which Dessalines had exhibited after the capture of Toussaint, the bold, resolute manner in which he had expelled the whites from the island, naturally pointed him out as the future ruler of St. Domingo. After serving a short time as president, Dessalines assumed the dignity of emperor, and changed the name of the island to that of Hayti.

The population of Hayti had been very much thinned by the ravages of war, and Dessalines, for the purpose of aiding those of his race, who had been taken away by force, to return, offered large rewards to captains of vessels for any that they might bring back as passengers.

One of the charges against Dessalines is based upon the fact that he changed his government from a republic to an empire. But we must consider that the people of Hayti had always lived under a monarchy, and were wedded to that kind of government. Had Toussaint allowed himself to be made a king, his power would have been recognized by Great Britain, and he would never have yielded to the solicitations of Leclerc, when that general's fleet landed on the island. Napoleon had just been crowned emperor of France, and it was not at all surprising that Dessalines should feel inclined to imitate the conqueror of Egypt.

The empire of Hayti was composed of six military divisions, each to be under the command of a general officer, who was independent of his associates who governed in other districts, as he was responsible to the head of the state alone. The supreme power was formally conferred upon Jean Jacques Dessalines, the avenger and liberator of his countrymen, who was to take the title of Emperor and Commander-in-chief of the Army, and to be addressed by the appellation of His Majesty--a dignity which was also conferred upon the empress, his wife, and the persons of both were declared inviolable. The crown was elective, but the power was conferred upon the reigning emperor to select and appoint his successor, by a nomination which required the sanction of the people to give it validity. The emperor was empowered to make the laws to govern the empire, and to promulgate them under his seal; to appoint all the functionaries of the state, and remove them at his will; to hold the purse of the nation; to make peace and war, and in all things to exercise the rights and privileges of an absolute sovereign. The monarch was assisted in wielding this mighty authority by a council of state, composed of generals of division and brigade. No peculiar faith in religion was established by law, and toleration was extended to the doctrines and worship of all sects. Surrounded by all the luxuries that wealth could procure, he was distinguished for the Roman virtues of abstinence and energy. Scorning effeminacy, he seemed ambitious to inure himself to the most laborious exercise and to the simplest mode of living. Dessalines was well schooled in the toils and labors of the camp. As his life was made up of extremes, so in his habits and personal endurances were seen great contrasts. Impetuosity and rapid movement were among his chief characteristics. He prided himself on his being able to surprise his enemies and taking them unprepared. Indeed, this was a leading trait in his military character, and places him alongside of Napoleon, or any other general, ancient or modern. As time smooths over his footsteps, and wears out the blood that marked his course, the circumstances attending it will, no doubt, be made to extenuate some of his many faults, and magnify his virtues as a general, a ruler, and a man.

The empress was a woman of rare beauty, and had some education, talent, and refinement. Her humanity caused her to restrain her husband, upon many occasions, from acts of cruelty. Though uneducated, Dessalines was not ignorant even of the classics, for he kept three secretaries, who, by turns, read to him.

As soon as he came into power, the emperor exerted every nerve to fortify the island, and to make it strong in the time of need. Much has been said of the cruelty of this man, and far be it from me to apologize for his acts. Yet, to judge rightly of him, we must remember that he had an ignorant people to govern, on the one hand, and the former planters to watch and control on the other. This latter class was scattered all over Europe and the United States, and they lost no opportunity to poison the minds of the whites against Dessalines and his government. He discovered many plots of the old white planters to assassinate him, and this drew out the ferociousness of his disposition, and made him cruel in the extreme. That he caused the death of innocent persons, there is not the slightest doubt; but that such a man as he was needed at the time, all must admit. Had Dessalines been in the place of Toussaint, he would never have been transferred from Hayti to France. Unlimited power, conferred upon him, together with the opposition of the whites in all countries, made him cruel even to his own race, and they looked forward with a degree of hope to his removal. The mulattoes, against whom he had never ceased to war, were ever watchful for an opportunity to take his life. A secret conspiracy was accordingly planned by this class, and on the 17th of October, 1806, while Dessalines was on a journey from St. Marks to Port au Prince, a party in ambuscade fired at him, and he fell dead.

Hayti had much improved under his management, especially in agriculture. The towns, many of them, had been rebuilt, commerce extended, and the arts patronized. Military talents have been ascribed to Dessalines even superior to Toussaint. He certainly had great courage, but upon the battle field it seemed to be the headlong fury of the tiger rather than the calm deliberation of L'Ouverture. Of all the heroic men which the boiling caldron of the St. Domingo revolution threw upon its surface, for the purpose of meeting the tyrannical whites, of bringing down upon them terrible retribution for their long and cruel reign, and of vindicating the rights of the oppressed in that unfortunate island, the foremost place belongs to the African, the savage, the soldier, the general, the president, and lastly the emperor Jean Jacques Dessalines.

## IRA ALDRIDGE.

ON looking over the columns of The Times, one morning, I saw it announced under the head of "Amusements," that "Ira Aldridge, the African Roscius," was to appear in the character of Othello, in Shakspeare's celebrated tragedy of that name, and, having long wished to see my sable countryman, I resolved at once to attend. Though the doors had been open but a short time when I reached the Royal Haymarket, the theatre where the performance was to take place, the house was well filled, and among the audience I recognized the faces of several distinguished persons of the nobility, the most noted of whom was Sir Edward Bulwer Lytton, the renowned novelist--his figure neat, trim, hair done up in the latest fashion--looking as if he had just come out of a band-box. He is a great lover of the drama, and has a private theatre at one of his country seats, to which he often invites his friends, and presses them into the different characters.

As the time approached for the curtain to rise, it was evident that the house was to be "jammed." Stuart, the best Iago since the days of Young, in company with Roderigo, came upon the stage as soon as the green curtain went up. Iago looked the villain, and acted it to the highest conception of the character. The scene is changed, all eyes are turned to the right door, and thunders of applause greet the appearance of Othello. Mr. Aldridge is of the middle size, and appeared to be about three quarters African; has a pleasant countenance, frame well knit, and seemed to me the best Othello that I had ever seen. As Iago began to work upon his feelings, the Moor's eyes flashed fire, and, further on in the play, he looked the very demon of despair. When he seized the deceiver by the throat, and exclaimed, "Villain! be sure thou prove my love false: be sure of it--give me the ocular proof--or, by the worth of my eternal soul, thou hadst better have been born a dog, Iago, than answer my waked wrath," the audience, with one impulse, rose to their feet amid the wildest enthusiasm. At the end of the third act, Othello was called before the curtain, and received the applause of the delighted multitude. I watched the countenance and every motion of Bulwer Lytton with almost as much interest as I did that of the Moor of Venice, and saw that none appeared to be better pleased than he. The following evening I went to witness his Hamlet, and was surprised to find him as perfect in that as he had been in Othello; for I had been led to believe that the latter was his greatest character. The whole court of Denmark was before us; but till the words, "'Tis not alone my inky cloak, good mother," fell from the lips of Mr. Aldridge, was the general ear charmed, or the general tongue arrested. The voice was so low, and sad, and sweet, the modulation so tender, the dignity so natural, the grace so consummate, that all yielded themselves silently to the delicious enchantment. When Horatio told him that he had come to see his father's funeral, the deep melancholy that took possession of his face showed the great dramatic power of Mr. Aldridge. "I pray thee do not mock me, fellow-student," seemed to come from his inmost soul. The animation with which his countenance was lighted up, during Horatio's recital of the visits that the ghost had paid him and his companions, was beyond description. "Angels and ministers of grace defend us," as the ghost appeared in the fourth scene, sent a thrill through the whole assembly. His rendering of the "Soliloquy on Death," which Edmund Kean, Charles Kemble, and William C. Macready have reaped such unfading laurels from, was one of his best efforts. He read it infinitely better than Charles Kean, whom I had heard at the "Princess," but a few nights previous. The vigorous starts of thought, which in the midst of his personal sorrows rise with such beautiful and striking suddenness from the ever-wakeful mind of the humanitarian philosopher, are delivered with that varying emphasis that characterizes the truthful delineator, when he exclaims, "Frailty, thy name is woman!" In the second scene of the second act, when revealing to Guildenstern the melancholy which preys upon his mind, the beautiful and powerful words in which Hamlet explains his feelings are made very effective in Mr. Aldridge's rendering: "This most excellent canopy, the air, the brave o'erhanging firmament, this majestical roof fretted with golden fire . . . . What a piece of work is a man! How noble in reason! how infinite in faculties! in form and moving how express and admirable! in action how like an angel! in apprehension how like a God!" In the last scene of the second act, when Hamlet's imagination, influenced by the interview with the actors, suggests to his rich mind so many eloquent reflections, Mr. Aldridge enters fully into the spirit of the scene, warms up, and when he exclaims, "He would drown the stage with tears, and cleave the general ear with horrid speech,--make mad the guilty, and appall the free," he is very effective; and when this warmth mounts into a paroxysm of rage, and he calls the King "Bloody, bawdy villain! Remorseless, treacherous, lecherous, kindless villain!" he sweeps the audience with him, and brings down deserved applause. The fervent soul and restless imagination, which are ever stirring at the bottom of the fountain, and sending bright bubbles to the top, find a glowing reflection on the animated surface of Mr. Aldridge's colored face. I thought Hamlet one of his best characters, though I saw him afterwards in several others.

Mr. Aldridge is a native of Senegal, in Africa. His forefathers were princes of the Foulah tribe, whose dominions were in Senegal, on the banks of the river of that name, on the west coast of Africa. To this shore one of our early missionaries found his way, and took charge of Ira's father, Daniel Aldridge, in order to qualify him for the work of civilizing and evangelizing his countrymen. Daniel's father, the reigning prince, was more enlightened than his subjects, probably through the instruction of the missionary, and proposed that his prisoners taken in battle should be exchanged, and not, as was the custom, sold as slaves. This wish interfered with the notions and perquisites of his tribe, especially his principal chiefs; and a civil war raged among the people. During these differences, Daniel, then a promising youth, was brought to the United States by the missionary, and sent to Schenectady College to receive the advantages of a Christian education. Three days after his departure, the revolutionary storm, which was brewing, broke out openly, and the reigning prince, the advocate of humanity, was killed.

Daniel Aldridge remained in America till the death of the rebellious chief, who had headed the conspiracy, and reigned instead of the murdered prince. During the interval, Daniel had become a minister of the gospel, and was regarded by all classes as a man of uncommon abilities. He was, however, desirous to establish himself at the head of his tribe, possess himself of his birthright, and advance the cause of Christianity among his countrymen. For this purpose he returned to his native country, taking with him a young wife, one of his own color, whom he had but just married in America. Daniel no sooner appeared among the people of his slaughtered father, than old disagreements revived, civil war broke out, the enlightened African was defeated, barely escaping from the scene of strife with his life, and for some time unable to quit the country, which was watched by numerous enemies anxious for his capture. Nine years elapsed before the proscribed family escaped to America, during the whole of which time they were concealed in the neighborhood of their foes, enduring vicissitudes and hardships that can well be imagined, but need not be described.

Ira Aldridge was born soon after his father's arrival in Senegal, and on their return to America, was intended by the latter for the church. Many a white parent has "chalked out" in vain for his son a similar calling, and the best intentions have been thwarted by an early predilection quite in an opposite direction. We can well account for the father's choice in this instance, as in keeping with his own aspirations; and we can easily imagine his disappointment upon abandoning all hope of seeing one of his blood and color following specially in the service of his great Master. The son, however, began betimes to show his early preference and ultimate passion. At school he was awarded prizes for declamation, in which he excelled; and there his curiosity was excited by what he heard of theatrical representations, which he was told embodied all the fine ideas shadowed forth in the language he read and committed to memory. It became the wish of his heart to witness one of these performances, and that wish he soon contrived to gratify, and finally he became a candidate for histrionic fame.

Notwithstanding the progress Ira had made in learning, no qualities of the mind could compensate, in the eyes of the Americans, for the dark hue of his skin. The prevailing prejudice, so strong among all classes, was against him. This induced his removal to England, where he entered at the Glasgow University, and, under Professor Sandford, obtained several premiums, and the medal for Latin composition.

On leaving college, Mr. Aldridge at once commenced preparing for the stage, and shortly after appeared in a number of Shaksperian characters, in Edinburgh, Glasgow, Manchester, and other provincial cities, and soon after appeared on the boards of Drury Lane and Covent Garden, where he was stamped the "African Roscius." The London Weekly Times said of him, "Mr. Ira Aldridge is a dark mulatto, with woolly hair. His features are capable of great expression, his action is unrestrained and picturesque, and his voice clear, full, and resonant. His powers of energetic declamation are very marked, and the whole of his acting appears impulsed by a current of feeling of no inconsiderable weight and vigor, yet controlled and guided in a manner that clearly shows the actor to be a person of much study and great stage ability." The Morning Chronicle recorded his "Shylock" as among the "finest pieces of acting that a London audience had witnessed since the days of the elder Kean."

# JOSEPH CINQUE.

IN the month of August, 1839, there appeared in the newspapers a shocking story--that a schooner, going coastwise from Havana to Neuvitas, in the island of Cuba, early in July, with about twenty white passengers, and a large number of slaves, had been seized by the slaves in the night time, and the passengers and crew all murdered except two, who made their escape to land in an open boat. About the 20th of the same month, a strange craft was seen repeatedly on our coast, which was believed to be the captured Spanish coaster, in the possession of the negroes. She was spoken by several pilot-boats and other vessels, and partially supplied with water, of which she was very much in want. It was also said that the blacks appeared to have a great deal of money. The custom-house department and the officers of the navy were instantly roused to go in pursuit of the "pirates," as the unknown possessors of the schooner were spontaneously called. The United States steamer Fulton, and several revenue cutters were despatched, and notice given to the collectors at the various seaports. On the 10th of August, the "mysterious schooner" was near the shore at Culloden Point, on the east end of Long Island, where a part of the crew came on shore for water and fresh provisions, for which they paid with undiscriminating profuseness. Here they were met by Captain Green and another gentleman, who stated that they had in their possession a large box filled with gold. Shortly after, on the 26th, the vessel was espied by Captain Gedney, U. S. N., in command of the brig Washington, employed on the coast survey, who despatched an officer to board her. The officer found a large number of negroes, and two Spaniards, Pedro Montez and Jose Ruiz, one of whom immediately announced himself as the owner of the negroes, and claimed his protection. The schooner was thereupon taken possession of by Captain Gedney.

The leader of the blacks was pointed out by the Spaniards, and his name given as Joseph Cinque. he was a native of Africa, and one of the finest specimens of his race ever seen in this country. As soon as he saw that the vessel was in the hands of others, and all hope of his taking himself and countrymen back to their home land at an end, he leaped overboard with the agility of an antelope. The small boat was immediately sent after him, and for two hours did the sailors strive to capture him before they succeeded. Cinque swam and dived like an otter, first upon his back, then upon his breast, sometimes his head out of water, and sometimes his heels out. His countrymen on board the captured schooner seemed much amused at the chase, for they knew Cinque well, and felt proud of the untamableness of his nature. After baffling them for a time, he swam towards the vessel, was taken on board, and secured with the rest of the blacks, and they were taken into New London, Connecticut.

The schooner proved to be the "Amistad," Captain Ramon Ferrer, from Havana, bound to Principe, about one hundred leagues distant, with fifty-four negroes held as slaves, and two passengers instead of twenty. The Spaniards said that, after being out four days, the negroes rose in the night, and killed the captain and a mulatto cook; that the helmsman and another sailor took to the boat and went on shore; that the only two whites remaining were the said passengers, Montez and Ruiz, who were confined below until morning; that Montez, the elder, who had been a sea captain, was required to steer the ship for Africa; that he steered eastwardly in the day time, because the negroes could tell his course by the sun, but put the vessel about in the night. They boxed about some days in the Bahama Channel, and were several times near the islands, but the negroes would not allow her to enter any port. Once they were near Long Island, but then put out to sea again, the Spaniards all the while hoping they might fall in with some ship of war that would rescue them from their awkward situation. One of the Spaniards testified that, when the rising took place, he was awaked by the noise, and that he heard the captain order the cabin boy to get some bread and throw to the negroes, in hope to pacify them. Cinque, however, the leader of the revolt, leaped on deck, seized a capstan bar, and attacked the captain, whom he killed at a single blow, and took charge of the vessel; his authority being acknowledged by his companions, who knew him as a prince in his native land.

The captives were taken before the Circuit Court of the United States for the District of Connecticut, Hon. Andrew T. Judson presiding. This was only the commencement in the courts, for the trial ran through several months. During this time, the Africans were provided with competent teachers by the abolitionists, and their minds were undergoing a rapid change, and civilization was taking the place of ignorance and barbarism.

Cinque, all this while, did nothing to change the high opinion first formed of him, and all those who came into his presence felt themselves before a superior man. After he and his countrymen had embraced Christianity, and were being questioned by a peace man as to the part that they had taken in the death of the men on board the Amistad, when asked if they did not think it wrong to take human life, one of the Africans replied that, if it was to be acted over again, he would pray for them instead of killing them; Cinque, hearing this, smiled and shook his head, whereupon he was asked if he would not pray for them also. To this he said, "Yes, I would pray for 'em, an' kill 'em too."

By the sagacity and daring of this man, he and his companions, fifty-four in number, were rescued from a life-long bondage of the worst character that ever afflicted the human family.

Cinque was a man of great intelligence and natural ability; he was a powerful orator, and although speaking in a tongue foreign to his audience, by the grace and energy of his motions and attitudes, the changeful expression of his features, and the intonations of his voice, made them understand the main incidents of his narrative, and swayed their minds in an extraordinary manner. Alluding to that point of his history at which Cinque described how, when on board the Spanish vessel, he, with the help of a nail, first relieved himself of his manacles, then assisted his countrymen to get rid of theirs, and then led them to the attack of the Spaniards, Lewis Tappan, in the account of the whole proceedings connected with the Amistad captives, which he published, says, "It is not in my power to give an adequate description of Cinque when he showed how he did this, and led his comrades to the conflict, and achieved their freedom. In my younger years I have seen Kemble and Siddons, and the representation of 'Othello,' at Covent Garden; but no acting that I have ever witnessed came near that to which I allude."

## ALEXANDRE DUMAS.

I HAD been in Paris a week without seeing Dumas, for my letter of introduction from Louis Blanc, who was then in exile in England, to M. Eugene Sue, had availed me nothing as regarded a sight of the great colored author. Sue had promised me that I should have an interview with Dumas before I quitted the French capital; but I had begun to suspect that the latter felt that it would be too much of a condescension to give audience to an American slave, and I began to grow indifferent myself upon the matter. Invited by a friend to attend the opera, to witness the performances of Grisi and Mario, in Norma, I gladly accepted, and in company with my friend started for the place of amusement. Our seats were "reserved," and I took my place in the immense saloon before raising my eyes to view the vast audience which had already assembled. The splendid chandeliers, the hundreds of brilliant gas lights, the highly-colored drapery that hung its rich folds about the boxes and stalls, were in keeping with the magnificent diamonds, laces, and jewelry, that adorned the persons of the finest assembly that I had ever seen. In a double box nearly opposite to me, containing a party of six or eight, I noticed a light-complexioned mulatto, apparently about fifty years of age,--curly hair, full face, dressed in a black coat, white vest, white kids,--who seemed to be the centre of attraction, not only in his own circle, but in others. Those in the pit looked up, those in the gallery looked down, while curtains were drawn aside at other boxes and stalls to get a sight at the colored man. So recently from America, where caste was so injurious to my race, I began to think that it was his woolly head that attracted attention, when I was informed that the mulatto before me was no less a person than Alexandre Dumas. Every move, look, and gesture of the celebrated romancer were watched in the closest manner by the audience. Even Mario appeared to feel that his part on the stage was of less importance than that of the colored man in the royal box. M. Dumas' grandfather was the Marquis de la Pailleterie, a wealthy planter of St. Domingo, while his grandmother was a negress from Congo.

Rainsford makes honorable mention of the father of Dumas, in his Black Empire, as having served in the army in his own native island. Dumas' father served under Napoleon during the whole of his campaigns, and rose to high distinction. Once, when near Lisle, Dumas, with four men, attacked a post of fifty Austrians, killed six, and made sixteen prisoners. For a long time he commanded a legion of horse composed of blacks and mulattoes, who were the terror of their enemies. General Dumas was with the army which Napoleon sent over the Alps; Napoleon crossed it in June, Marshal Macdonald in December. The latter sent Dumas to say it was impossible to pass in the winter, when great avalanches of snow were falling down, threatening to destroy the army. Napoleon's reply to the messenger was, "Go and tell Marshal Macdonald, where one man can pass over, an army can pass over in single file. The order is not to be countermanded." The order was obeyed, though at the cost of many lives. One of the generals that made the pass was the black General Dumas, who ascended the St. Bernard, which was defended by a number of fortifications, took possession of the cannon, and immediately directed them against the enemy. At the conclusion of the wars, the father returned to his island home, and after his death, the son went to France destitute, where he obtained a situation as a writer. Here he cultivated his literary taste. His imaginative mind and unsurpassed energies began to develop themselves, which soon placed the young man in easy circumstances. Dumas is now sixty-three years of age, and has been a writer for the press thirty-eight years. During this time he has published more novels, plays, travels, and historical sketches than any other man that ever lived. It is well understood that he is not the author of all the works that appear under his name, but that young writers gain a living by working out the plots and situations that his fecund brain suggests. When the novel or the play is complete, Dumas gives it a revision, touches up the dialogue, dashes in here and there a spirited scene of his own, and then receives from the publisher an enormous sum. Undeniably a man of great genius, endowed with true fertility of imagination, and masterly power of expression, his influence has been great.

Such is the vivacity of his descriptions, such the entrainement of his narrative, such the boldness of his invention, such the point of his dialogue, and the rapidity of his incidents, so matchless often the felicity and skill of particular passages, that he always inflames the interest of the reader to the end. You may be angry with him, but you will confess that he is the opposite of tedious. Certainly no writer fills a more prominent place in the literature of his country; and none has exercised a more potent influence upon its recent development than this son of the negro general, Dumas. His novels are every where, and the enthusiasm with which his dramatic pieces were received has been of the most flattering character.

## HENRI CHRISTOPHE.

HENRI CHRISTOPHE was a native of the island of New Grenada, where be was born a slave. He went to St. Domingo at the age of eighteen, and was employed as maître d'hôtel in the principal café at Cape François. From strength of natural genius, as well as from his occupying a station in life above the ordinary condition of his race, he acquired considerable knowledge of the prevailing manners and customs of the society of which he was a daily spectator. He was master of the French, English, and Spanish languages, and was thought to be the most polished gentleman of all of Toussaint's generals. Being six feet three inches in height, Christophe made an imposing appearance on horseback, on the field of battle, in his uniform. He had a majestic carriage, and an eye full of fire; and a braver man never lived. Though far inferior to Toussaint in vigor and originality of mind, he was much his superior in acquaintance with the customs and habits of the world, and appeared more dignified in his intercourse with society.

After the breaking out of the revolution, Christophe joined the army under Toussaint, who soon discovered his good qualities, and made him his lieutenant; from which position he was soon advanced to second in command. It has been asserted that he was an abler military man than either Toussaint or Dessalines. When Napoleon's expedition invaded St. Domingo, Leclerc, with the largest part of the squadron, came to anchor off Cape City, and summoned the place to surrender.

The reply which he received from Christophe was such as to teach the captain-general what he had to expect in the subjugation of St. Domingo. "Go, tell your general that the French shall march here only over ashes, and that the ground shall burn beneath their feet," was the answer that Leclerc obtained in return to his command. The French general sent another messenger to Christophe, urging him to surrender, and promising the black chief a commission of high rank in the French army. But he found he had a man, and not a slave, to deal with. The exasperated Christophe sent back the heroic reply, "The decision of arms can admit you only into a city in ashes, and even on these ashes will I fight still."

After Toussaint had been captured and sent to France, and Leclerc was disarming the colored population, and the decree of the 30th of April for maintaining slavery in St. Domingo had been put forth, Christophe followed the example of Clervaux, and went over to the insurgents, and met and defeated Rocbambeau in one of the hardest fought battles of the campaign. He soon after shut the French commander up in Cape Francois, where the latter remained like a tiger driven to his den.

During the reign of Dessalines, Christophe lived partly retired, "biding his time;" for although the former had been made emperor, the latter was most beloved by all classes. The death of the emperor at once opened a way for Christophe, for a provisional government was then constituted, and the latter was proclaimed the head of the state. This was a virtual revolution, and Christophe regarded himself, by the provisional appointment, as the chief of the army, to govern ad interim, until a new government could be formed. But the mulattoes, who had long been in obscurity, rallied, got a majority in the convention, and elected Petion president of the republic of Hayti. Christophe collected together his adherents, and determined to take by conquest what he thought he had a right to by succession, and, as he thought, by merit. Failing in this, he set up another government in the north, with Cape François as its capital. Christophe felt that his assumption of power was but a usurpation, and that, so long as his government remained in operation without the formal sanction of the people, his rival at Port au Prince possessed immense advantage over him, inasmuch as he had been made the constituted head of the country by an observance of the forms of the constitution. To remedy this palpable defect, which weakened his authority, he resolved to frame another constitution, which would confirm him in the power he had taken, and furnish him with a legal excuse for maintaining his present attitude. In accordance with this policy, he convoked another assembly at Cape François, composed of the generals of his army and the principal citizens of that province, and after a short session the legislators terminated their labors by adopting another constitution, dated upon the 17th of February, 1809. This new enactment declared all persons residing upon the territory of Hayti free citizens, and that the government was to be administered by a supreme magistrate, who was to take the title of president of the state and general-in-chief of the land and naval forces. Thus firmly seated, Christophe felt himself more powerful, and more secure from outbreaks. Nevertheless, he was not destined to hold peaceable possession of all the territory in his district, for the inhabitants of many of the towns in the vicinity of Cape François openly threw off their allegiance, and proclaimed their preference for the more legitimate government of Petion. The two presidents prepared for war, and Christophe opened the campaign by marching an immense army against Gonaives, which, in the month of June, 1807, he invested. Petion's troops were defeated, and, to save themselves from capture, escaped by sea to Port au Prince. The war continued three years, when a new competitor appeared in the person of Rigaud, the other mulatto general. Christophe now ceased for a while; but when he felt that the time had arrived he again renewed the war, and, in 1810, captured the Mole St. Nicholas, the strongest fort on the island. Becoming ambitious to be a monarch, Christophe called his council together, and on the 20th of March, 1811, the session closed by adopting a new frame of government. The imperial constitution of 1805 was modified to form an hereditary monarchy in the north, and to place the crown of Hayti upon Christophe, under the title of Henry the First. When he entered upon the kingly station that had been conferred upon him, his first act was to promulgate an edict creating an hereditary nobility, as a natural support of his government. These dignitaries of the kingdom were taken mostly from the army, the chiefs who had fought under him in the struggle against the French, and consisted of two princes, seven dukes, twenty-two counts, thirty-five barons, and fourteen chevaliers. His coronation was the most magnificent display ever witnessed out of Europe. To furnish himself with all the appointments correspondent to his royal dignity, he now began the erection of a palace, situated a few miles from the cape, upon which he had bestowed the historical name of Sans Souci. This palace has the reputation of being the most splendid edifice in the West Indies. The rugged, mountainous region in the vicinity of his royal residence was changed from its original condition to form the gardens of the palace. Hills were levelled with the plain, deep ravines were filled up, and roads and passages were opened, leading in all directions from the royal dwelling. The halls and saloons of the palace were wrought with mahogany, the floors were laid with rich marble, and numerous jets-d'eau furnished coolness and a supply of pure water to the different apartments. Christophe held a levee on the Thursday evening of each week, which was attended by the most fashionable of all classes, including the foreign ambassadors and consuls. The ceremonial observances were modelled after the drawing rooms at St. Cloud and St. James. Though of pure African blood, Christophe was not a jet black, his complexion being rather a dusky brown. His person had grown slightly corpulent, and his address was cold, polished, and graceful. He possessed a certain air of native dignity that corresponded well with his high official situation. The whites of all countries, and especially the English, formed a high opinion of his character. That part of the island which came within his rule had been well cultivated, his government out of debt, and commerce was in a flourishing condition.

The removal of Napoleon from the throne of France once more gave to the French planters residing in the mother country hope of again possessing their estates.
A move was made in the court of Louis XVIII. to send another expedition to Hayti, to bring the colony back to her allegiance. On learning this, Christophe issued a proclamation, in which he said, "If we love the blessings of peace, we fear not the fatigues and horrors of war. Let our implacable enemies, the French colonists, who for twenty years have never ceased from their projects for the reestablishment of slavery, and who have filled all the governments of the earth with their importunities,--let them put themselves at the head of armies, and direct themselves against our country. They will be the first victims of our vengeance, and the soil of liberty will eagerly drink the blood of our oppressors. We will show to the nations of the earth what a warlike people can accomplish, who are in arms for the best of causes--the defence of their homes, their wives, their children, their liberty, and their independence."

A despatch was next sent to Christophe, in which he was threatened with an invasion by all the forces of combined Europe in case of his refusal to submit himself to the will of France. This last threat, however, had no influence over the black monarch, for he felt that no European power would invade Hayti after the failure of the sixty thousand men sent out by Napoleon. Nothing was attempted by the French, and the king of Hayti was left in possession of his government. In the month of August, 1820, Christophe was attacked, while at mass, with a paralytic disease, and was immediately conveyed to Sans Souci, where he remained an invalid until a revolt occurred among his subjects. He ordered his war-horse, his sword was brought, and he attempted to mount his charger; but in vain. He gave up the attempt, retired to his chamber, locked the door, and the report of a pistol alarmed his attendants. They rushed in, but it was too late; Henri Christophe was no more.

Christophe's aims were great, and many of them good. He was not only the patron of the arts, but of industry; and it gave him pleasure to see his country recovering the ground lost in the revolution and the civil wars, and advancing in name and wealth. He promoted industry on the principles laid down by his predecessor, Toussaint. A busy population covered the land with marks of its labors. Rich crops of the most coveted produce of nature annually rewarded the toil of the husbandman. Christophe was also the patron of education; and there are still on the island schools that were founded by him when king. In one respect he excelled Charlemagne,--he could write his own name; but that was all. He dictated letters and despatches, and was an admirable judge of the fitness and relevancy of words. He kept up a correspondence with Wilberforce and Clarkson, the English philanthropists, and both of these distinguished men had a high opinion of him as a man, and a friend of his race.

# PHILLIS WHEATLEY.

IN the year 1761, when Boston had her slave market, and the descendants of the Pilgrims appeared to be the most pious and God-fearing people in the world, Mrs. John Wheatley went into the market one day, for the purpose of selecting and purchasing a girl for her own use. Among the group of children just imported from the African coast was a delicately built, rather good-looking child of seven or eight years, apparently suffering from the recent sea voyage and change of climate. Mrs. Wheatley's heart was touched at the interesting countenance and humble modesty of this little stranger. The lady bought the child, and she was named Phillis. Struck with the slave's uncommon brightness, the mistress determined to teach her to read, which she did with no difficulty. The child soon mastered the English language, with which she was totally unacquainted when she landed upon the American shores. Her school lessons were all perfect, and she drank in the scriptural teachings as if by intuition. At the age of twelve, she could write letters and keep up a correspondence that would have done honor to one double her years. Mrs. Wheatley, seeing her superior genius, no longer regarded Phillis as a servant, but took her as a companion. It was not surprising that the slave girl should be an object of attraction, astonishment, and attention with the refined and highly cultivated society that weekly assembled in the drawing room of the Wheatleys. As Phillis grew up to womanhood, her progress and attainments kept pace with the promise of her earlier years. She drew around her the best educated of the white ladies, and attracted the attention and notice of the literary characters of Boston, who supplied her with books and encouraged the ripening of her intellectual powers. She studied the Latin tongue, and translated one of Ovid's tales, which was no sooner put in print in America, than it was republished in London, with eloquent commendations from the reviews. In 1773, a small volume of her poems, containing thirty-nine pieces, was published in London, and dedicated to the Countess of Huntingdon. The genuineness of this work was established in the first page of the volume, by a document signed by the governor of Massachusetts, the lieutenant-governor, her master, and fifteen of the most respectable and influential citizens of Boston, who were acquainted with her talents and the circumstances of her life. Her constitution being naturally fragile, she was advised by her physician to take a sea voyage as the means of restoring her declining health.

Phillis was emancipated by her master at the age of twenty-one years, and sailed for England. On her arrival, she was received and admired in the first circles of London society; and it was at that time that her poems were collected and published in a volume, with a portrait and memoir of the authoress. Phillis returned to America, and married Dr. Peters, a man of her own color, and of considerable talents. Her health began rapidly to decline, and she died at the age of twenty-six years, in 1780. Fortunately rescued from the fate that awaits the victims of the slave trade, this injured daughter of Africa had an opportunity of developing the genius that God had given her, and of showing to the world the great wrong done to her race. The limited place allowed for this sketch will not permit of our giving more than one short poem from the pen of the gifted Phillis Wheatley.

## ON THE DEATH OF A YOUNG GIRL.

From dark abodes to fair ethereal light,
The enraptured innocent has winged her flight;
On the kind bosom of eternal love
She finds unknown beatitudes above.
This know, ye parents, nor her loss deplore--
She feels the iron hand of pain no more;
The dispensations of unerring grace
Should turn your sorrows into grateful praise;
Let, then, no tears for her henceforward flow
Nor stiffer grief in this dark vale below.

Her morning sun, which rose divinely bright,
Was quickly mantled with the gloom of night;
But hear, in heaven's best bowers, your child so fair,
And learn to imitate her language there.
Thou, Lord, whom I behold with glory crowned,
By what sweet name, and in what tuneful sound,
Wilt thou be praised? Seraphic powers are faint
Infinite love and majesty to paint.
To thee let all their grateful voices raise,
And saints and angels join their songs of praise

Perfect in bliss, now from her heavenly home
She looks, and, smiling, beckons you to come;
Why then, fond parents, why these fruitless groans?
Restrain your tears, and cease your plaintive moans.
Freed from a world of sin, and snares, and pain,
Why would ye wish your fair one back again?
Nay, bow resigned; let hope your grief control,
And check the rising tumult of the soul.
Calm in the prosperous and the adverse day,
Adore the God who gives and takes away;

See him in all, his holy name revere,
Upright your actions, and your hearts sincere,
Till, having sailed through life's tempestuous sea,
And from its rocks and boisterous billows free,
Yourselves, safe landed on the blissful shore,
Shall join your happy child to part no more.

## DENMARK VESEY.

No class of persons in the world, who have the name of being free, are more sorely oppressed than the free colored people of the Southern States. Each state has its code of black laws, which are rigorously enforced, and the victim made to feel his degradation at all times and in all places. An undeveloped discontent pervades the entire black population, bond and free, in all the slave states. Human bondage is ever fruitful of insurrection, wherever it exists, and under whatever circumstances it may be found. Every community the other side of "Dixon's Line" feels that it lives upon a volcano that is liable to burst out at any moment; and all are watchful, and fearfully in earnest, in looking after the colored man's affairs, and inventing sterner enactments to keep him in subjection. The most oppressive of all the states is South Carolina. In Charleston, free colored ladies are not allowed to wear veils about their faces in the streets, or in any public places. A violation of this law is visited with "thirty-nine lashes upon the bare back." The same is inflicted upon any free colored man who shall be seen upon the streets with a cigar in his mouth,or a walking stick in his band. Both, when walking the streets, are forbidden to take the inside of the pavement. Punishment of fine and imprisonment is laid upon any found out after the hour of nine at night. An extra tax is placed upon every member of a free colored family. While all these odious edicts were silently borne by the free colored people of Charleston in 1822 there was a suppressed feeling of indignation, mortification, and discontent, that was only appreciated by a few. Among the most dissatisfied of the free blacks was Denmark Vesey, a man who had purchased his freedom in the year 1800, and since that time had earned his living by his trade, being a carpenter and joiner. Having been employed on shipboard by his master, Captain Vesey, Denmark had soon a great deal of the world, and had acquired a large fund of information, and was regarded as a leading man among the blacks. He had studied the Scriptures, and never lost an opportunity of showing that they were opposed to chattel-slavery. He spoke freely with the slaves upon the subject, and often with whites, where he found he could do so without risk to his own liberty. After resolving to incite the slaves to rebellion, he began taking into his confidence such persons as be could trust, and instructing them to gain adherents from among the more reliable of both bond and free. Peter Poyas, a slave of more than ordinary foresight and ability, was selected by Vesey as his lieutenant; and to him was committed the arduous duty of arranging the mode of attack, and of acting as the military leader.

"His plans showed some natural generalship; he arranged the night attack; he planned the enrolment of a mounted troop to scour the streets; and he had a list of all the shops where arms and ammunition were kept for sale. He voluntarily undertook the management of the most difficult part of the enterprise,--the capture of the main guard-house,--and had pledged himself to advance alone and surprise the sentinel. He was said to have a magnetism in his eye, of which his confederates stood in great awe; if he once got his eye upon a man, there was no resisting it."

Gullah Jack, Tom Russell, and Ned Bennett. The last two were not less valuable than Peter Poyas; for Tom was an ingenious mechanic, and made battleaxes, pikes, and other instruments of death, with which to carry on the war. All of the above were to be generals of brigades, and were let into all the secrets of the intended rising. It has long been the custom in Charleston for the country slaves to visit the city in great numbers on Sunday, and return to their homes in time to commence work on the following morning. It was therefore determined by Denmark to have the rising take place on Sunday. The slaves of nearly every plantation in the vicinity were enlisted, and were to take part.

"The details of the plan, however, were not rashly committed to the mass of the confederates; they were known only to a few, and were finally to have been announced after the evening prayer-meeting on the appointed Sunday. But each leader had his own company enlisted, and his own work marked out. When the clock struck twelve, all were to move. Peter Poyas was to lead a party ordered to assemble at South Bay, and to be joined by a force from James's Island; he was then to march up and seize the arsenal and guard-house opposite St. Michael's Church, and detach a sufficient number to cut off all white citizens who should appear at the alarm posts. A second body of negroes, from the country and the Neck, headed by Ned Bennett, was to assemble on the Neck and seize the arsenal there. A third was to meet at Governor Bennett's Mills, under command of Rolla, another leader, and, after putting the governor and intendant to death, to march through the city, or be posted at Cannon's Bridge, thus preventing the inhabitants of Cannonsborough from entering the city. A fourth, partly from the country and partly from the neighboring localities in the city, was to rendezvous on Gadsden's Wharf and attack the upper guard-house. A fifth, composed of country and Neck negroes, was to assemble at Bulkley's farm, two miles and a half from the city, seize the upper powder magazine, and then march down; and a sixth was to assemble at Denmark Vesey's and obey his orders. A seventh detachment, under Gullah Jack, was to assemble in Boundary Street, at the head of King Street, to capture the arms of the Neck company of militia, and to take an additional supply from Mr. Duquercron's shop. The naval stores on Mey's Wharf were also to be attacked. Meanwhile a horse company, consisting of many draymen, hostlers, and butcher boys, was to meet at Lightwood's Alley, and then scour the streets to prevent the whites from assembling. Every white man coming out of his own door was to be killed, and, if necessary, the city was to be fired in several places--slow match for this purpose having been purloined from the public arsenal and placed in an accessible position."

The secret and plan of attack, however, were incautiously divulged to a slave named Devany, belonging to Colonel Prioleau, and he at once informed his master's family. The mayor, on getting possession of the facts, called the city council together for consultation. The investigation elicited nothing new, for the slaves persisted in their ignorance of the matter, and the authorities began to feel that they had been imposed upon by Devany and his informant, when another of the conspirators, being bribed, revealed what he knew. Arrests after arrests were made, and the Mayor's Court held daily examinations for weeks. After several weeks of incarceration, the accused, one hundred and twenty in number, were brought to trial: thirty-four were sentenced to transportation, twenty-seven acquitted by the court, twenty-five discharged without trial, and thirty-five condemned to death. With but two or three exceptions, all of the conspirators went to the gallows feeling that they had acted right, and died like men giving their lives for the cause of freedom. A report of the trial, written soon after, says of Denmark Vesey,--

"For several years before he disclosed his intentions to any one, he appears to have been constantly and assiduously engaged in endeavoring to embitter the minds of the colored population against the white. He rendered himself perfectly familiar with all those parts of the Scriptures which he thought he could pervert to his purpose, and would readily quote them to prove that slavery was contrary to the laws of God,--that slaves were bound to attempt their emancipation, however shocking and bloody might be the consequences, --and that such efforts would not only be pleasing to the Almighty, but were absolutely enjoined, and their success predicted, in the Scriptures. His favorite texts, when he addressed those of his own color, were Zechariah xiv. 1-3, and Joshua vi. 21; and in all his conversations he identified their situation with that of the Israelites. The number of inflammatory pamphlets on slavery brought into Charleston from some of our sister states within the last four years, (and once from Sierra Leone,) and distributed amongst the colored population of the city, for which there was a great facility, in consequence of the unrestricted intercourse allowed to persons of color between the different states in the Union, and the speeches in Congress of those opposed to the admission of Missouri into the Union, perhaps garbled and misrepresented, furnished him with ample means for inflaming the minds of the colored population of this state; and by distorting certain parts of those speeches, or selecting from them particular passages, he persuaded but too many that Congress had actually declared them free, and that they were held in bondage contrary to the laws of the land. Even whilst walking through the streets in company with another, he was not idle; for if his companion bowed to a white person, he would rebuke him, and observe that all men were born equal, and that he was surprised that any one would degrade himself by such conduct,--that he would never cringe to the whites, nor ought any one who had the feelings of a man. When answered, 'We are slaves,' he would sarcastically and indignantly reply, 'You deserve to remain slaves;' and if he were further asked, 'What can we do?' he would remark, 'Go and buy a spelling-book and read the fable of Hercules and the Wagoner,' which he would then repeat, and apply it to their situation. He also sought every opportunity of entering into conversation with white persons, when they could be overheard by negroes near by, especially in grog shops; during which conversation, he would artfully introduce some bold remark on slavery; and sometimes, when, from the character he was conversing with, he found he might be still bolder, he would go so far, that, had not his declarations in such situations been clearly proved, they would scarcely have been credited. He continued this course until some time after the commencement of the last winter; by which time he had not only obtained incredible influence amongst persons of color, but many feared him more than their owners, and, one of them declared, even more than his God."

The excitement which the revelations of the trial occasioned, and the continual fanning of the flame by the newspapers, were beyond description. Double guard in the city, the country patrol on horseback and on foot, the watchfulness that was observed on all plantations, showed the deep feeling of fear pervading the hearts of the slaveholders, not only in South Carolina, but the fever extended to the other Southern States, and all seemed to feel that a great crisis had been passed. And indeed, their fears seem not to have been without ground, for a more complicated plan for an insurrection could scarcely have been conceived. And many were of opinion that, the rising once begun, they would have taken the city and held it, and might have sealed the fate of slavery in the south. The best account of this whole matter is to be found in an able article in the Atlantic Monthly for June, 1861, from the pen of that eloquent friend of freedom T. W. Higginson, and to which I am indebted for the extracts contained in this memoir of Denmark Vesey.

## HENRY HIGHLAND GARNETT.

Though born a slave in the State of Maryland, Henry Highland Garnett is the son of an African chief, stolen from the coast of his native land. His father's family were all held as slaves till 1822, when they escaped to the north. In 1835, he became a member of Canaan Academy, New Hampshire. Three months after entering the school, it was broken up by a mob, who destroyed the building. Mr. Garnett afterwards entered Oneida Institute, New York, under the charge of that noble-hearted friend of man, Beriah Green, where he was treated with equality by the professors and his fellow-students. There he gained the reputation of a courteous and accomplished man, an able and eloquent debater, and a good writer. His first appearance as a public speaker was in 1837, in the city of New York, where his speech at once secured for him a standing among first-class orators. Mr. Garnett is in every sense of the term a progressive man. He is a strenuous advocate of freedom, temperance, education, and the religious, moral, and social elevation of his race. He is an acceptable preacher, evangelical in his profession. His discourses, though showing much thought and careful study, are delivered extemporaneously, and with good effect. Having complete command of his voice, he uses it with skill, never failing to fill the largest hall. One of the most noted addresses ever given by a colored man in this country was delivered by Mr. Garnett at the National Convention of Colored Americans, at Buffalo, New York, in 1843. None but those who heard that speech have the slightest idea of the tremendous influence which he exercised over the assembly. He spent some years over a church at Troy, and another at Geneva, New York, and in 1850 visited England, where he remained, lecturing, in different sections of the United Kingdom, upon American slavery, until 1852, we believe, when, being joined by his family, he went as a missionary to Jamaica. After spending three years among the people of that island, he returned to the United States, and is now settled over Shiloh Church, New York city. Mr. Garnett is about forty-five years of age, unadulterated in race, tall and commanding in appearance, has an eye that looks through you, and a clear, ringing voice. He has written considerably, and has edited one or two journals at different times, devoted to the elevation of his race. The following from his pen will give but a faint idea of Mr. Garnett's powers as a writer:--

"The woful volume of our history, as it now lies open to the world, is written with tears and bound with blood. As I trace it, my eyes ache and my heart is filled with grief. No other people have suffered so much, and none have been more innocent. If I might apostrophize that bleeding country, I would say, O Africa, thou hast bled, freely bled, at every pore. Thy sorrow has been mocked, and thy grief has not been heeded. Thy children are scattered over the whole earth, and the great nations have been enriched by them. The wild beasts of thy forests are treated with more mercy than they. The Libyan lion and the fierce tiger are caged, to gratify the curiosity of men, and the keeper's hands are not laid heavily upon them. But thy children are tortured, taunted, and hurried out of life by unprecedented cruelty. Brave men, formed in the divinest mould, are bartered, sold, and mortgaged. Stripped of every sacred right, they are scourged if they affirm that they belong to God. Women, sustaining the dear relation of mothers, are yoked with the horned cattle to till the soil, and their heart-strings are torn to pieces by cruel separations from their children. Our sisters, ever manifesting the purest kindness, whether in the wilderness of their fatherland, or amid the sorrows of the middle passage, or in crowded cities, are unprotected from the lust of tyrants. They have a regard for virtue, and they possess a sense of honor; but there is no respect paid to these jewels of noble character. Driven into unwilling concubinage, their offspring are sold by their Anglo-Saxon fathers. To them the marriage institution is but a name, for their despoilers break down the hymeneal altar, and scatter its sacred ashes on the winds.

"Our young men are brutalized in intellect, and their manly energies are chilled by the frosts of slavery. Sometimes they are called to witness the agonies of the mothers who bore them, writhing under the lash; and as if to fill to overflowing the already full cup of demonism, they are sometimes compelled to apply the lash with their own hands. Hell itself cannot over-match a deed like this; and dark damnation shudders as it sinks into its bosom, and seeks to hide itself from the indignant eye of God."

Mr. Garnett paid a second visit to England a few months since, for the purpose of creating an interest there in behalf of emigration to Central Africa.

## JAMES M. WHITFIELD.

THERE has long resided in Buffalo, New York, a barber, noted for his scholarly attainments and gentlemanly deportment. Men of the most polished refinement visit his saloon, and, while being shaved, take pleasure in conversing with him; and all who know him feel that he was intended by nature for a higher position in life. This is James M. Whitfield. He is a native of Massachusetts, and removed west some years since. We give a single extract from one of his poems.

> "How long, O gracious God, how long
> Shall power lord it over right?
> The feeble, trampled by the strong,
> Remain in slavery's gloomy night?
> In every region of the earth
> Oppression rules with iron power;
> And every man of sterling worth,
> Whose soul disdains to cringe or cower
> Beneath a haughty tyrant's nod,
> And, supplicating, kiss the rod
> That, wielded by oppression's might,
> Smites to the earth his dearest right,--
> The right to speak, and think, and feel,
> And spread his uttered thoughts abroad,
> To labor for the common weal,
> Responsible to none but God,--
> Is threatened with the dungeon's gloom,
> The felon's cell, the traitor's doom,
>
> And treacherous politicians league

With hireling priests to crush and ban
All who expose their vain intrigue,
And vindicate the rights of man.
How long shall Afric raise to thee
Her fettered hand, O Lord, in vain,
And plead in fearful agony
For vengeance for her children slain?
I see the Gambia's swelling flood,
And Niger's darkly-rolling wave,
Bear on their bosoms, stained with blood,
The bound and lacerated slave;
While numerous tribes spread near and far
Fierce, devastating, barbarous war,
Earth's fairest scenes in ruin laid,
To furnish victims for that trade
Which breeds on earth such deeds of shame,
As fiends might blush to hear or name."

Mr. Whitfield has written several long poems, all of them in good taste and excellent language.

## ANDRE RIGAUD.

SLAVERY, in St. Domingo, created three classes-- the white planters, the free mulattoes, and the slaves, the latter being all black. The revolution brought out several valiant chiefs among the mulattoes, their first being Vincent Oge. This man was not calculated for a leader of rebellion. His mother having been enabled to support him in France as a gentleman, he had cherished a delicacy of sentiment very incompatible with the ferocity of revolt. But Andre Rigaud, their next and greatest chief, was a far different man. A native of Aux Cayes, educated at Bourdeaux, and afterwards spending some time at Paris, maturing his mind amid scenes of science and literature, Rigaud's position among his followers was an exalted one. His father was white and his mother black. He was tall and slim, with features beautifully defined. Nature had been profligate in bestowing her gifts upon him.

While at the Military School at Paris, besides being introduced into good society, he became acquainted with Lafayette, Condorcet, Gregoire, and other distinguished statesmen, and his manners were polished and his language elegant. In religion he was the very opposite of Toussaint. An admirer of Voltaire and Rousseau, he had made their works his study. A long residence in the French metropolis had enabled him to become acquainted with the followers of these two distinguished philosophers. He had seen two hundred thousand persons following the bones of Voltaire, when removed to the Pantheon, and, in his admiration for the great author, had confounded liberty with infidelity. In Asia, he would have governed an empire; in St. Domingo, he was scarcely more than an outlawed chief; but be had in his soul the elements of a great man. In military science, horsemanship, and activity, Rigaud was the first man on the island, of any color. Toussaint bears the following testimony to the great skill of the mulatto general: "I know Rigaud well. He leaps from his horse when at full gallop, and he puts all his force in his arm when he strikes a blow." He was high-tempered, irritable, and haughty. The charmed power that he held over the men of his color can scarcely be described. At the breaking out of the revolution, he headed the mulattoes in his native town, and soon drew around him a formidable body of men.

After driving the English and Spaniards from the island, and subduing the French planters, Toussaint and Rigaud made war upon each other. As the mulattoes were less than fifty thousand in number, and the blacks more than five hundred thousand, Rigaud was always outnumbered on the field of battle; but his forces, fighting under the eyes of the general whom they adored, defended their territory with vigor, if not with success. Reduced in his means of defence by the loss of so many brave men in his recent battles, Rigaud had the misfortune to see his towns fall, one after another, into the power of Toussaint, until he was driven to the last citadel of his strength--the town of Aux Cayes. As he thus yielded foot by foot, every thing was given to desolation before it was abandoned, and the land, which under his active government had just before been so adorned with cultivation, was made such a waste of desolation, that, according almost to the very letter of his orders, "the trees were turned with their roots in the air." The genius and activity of Toussaint were completely at fault in his attempt to force the mulatto general from his intrenchments.

The government of France was too much engaged at home with her own revolution to pay any attention to St. Domingo. The republicans in Paris, after getting rid of their enemies, turned upon each other. The revolution, like Saturn, devoured its own children; priest and people were murdered upon the thresholds of justice. Murat died at the hands of Charlotte Corday. Louis XVI. and Marie Antoinette were guillotined, Robespierre had gone to the scaffold, and Bonaparte was master of France.

The conqueror of Egypt now turned his attention to St. Domingo. It was too important an island to be lost to France or destroyed by civil war, and, through the mediation of Bonaparte, the war between Toussaint and Rigaud was brought to a close.

Petion and several other generals followed Rigaud when, at the conclusion of his war with Toussaint, he embarked for France. When Napoleon's ill-fated expedition came to St. Domingo, Rigaud returned, made his appearance at Aux Cayes, and, under his influence, the south soon rallied in arms against Toussaint. He fought bravely for France until the subjugation of the blacks and the transportation of their chief to the mother country, when Napoleon felt that Rigaud, too, was as dangerous to the peace of St. Domingo as Toussaint, and he was once more forced to return to France. Here he was imprisoned--not for any thing that he had done against the government of Bonaparte, but for fear that the mulatto chief would return to his native island, take up arms, and assist his race, who were already in rebellion against Leclerc.

Although the whites and the free colored men were linked together by the tender ties of nature, there was, nevertheless, a hatred to each other, even stronger than between the whites and the blacks. In the earlier stages of the revolution, before the blacks under Toussaint got the ascendency, several attempts had been made to get rid of the leaders of the mulattoes, and especially Rigaud. He was hated by the whites in the same degree as they feared his all-powerful influence with his race, and the unyielding nature of his character, which gave firmness and consistency to his policy while controlling the interests of his brethren. Intrigue and craftiness could avail nothing against the designs of one who was ever upon the watch, and who had the means of counteracting all secret attempts against him; and open force, in the field, could not be successful in destroying a chieftain whose power was often felt, but whose person was seldom seen. Thus, to accomplish a design which had long been in meditation, the whites of Aux Cayes were now secretly preparing a mine for Rigaud, which, though it was covered with roses, and to be sprung by professed friends, it was thought would prove a sure and efficacious method of ridding them of such an opponent, and destroying the pretensions of the mulattoes forever. It was proposed that the anniversary of the destruction of the Bastile should be celebrated in the town by both whites and mulattoes, in union and gratitude. A civic procession marched to the church, where Te Deum was chanted and all oration pronounced. The Place d'Armes was crowded with tables of refreshments, at which both whites and mulattoes seated themselves. But beneath this seeming patriotism and friendship, a dark and fatal conspiracy lurked, plotting treachery and death. It had been resolved that, at a preconcerted signal, every white at the table should plunge his knife into the bosom of the mulatto who was seated nearest to him. Cannon had been planted around the place of festivity, that no fugitive from the massacre should have the means of escaping; and that Rigaud should not fail to be secured as the first victim of a conspiracy prepared especially against his life, the commander-in-chief of the National Guard had been placed at his side, and his murder of the mulatto chieftain was to be the signal for a general onset upon all his followers. The officer to whom had been intrusted the assassination of Rigaud, found it no small matter to screw his courage up to the sticking point, and the expected signal, which he was to display in blood to his associates, was so long delayed, that secret messengers began to throng to him from all parts of the tables, demanding why execution was not done on Rigaud. Urged on by these successive appeals, the white general at last applied himself to the fatal task which had been allotted him; but instead of silently plunging his dagger into the bosom of the mulatto chief, he sprung upon him with a pistol in his hand, and, with a loud execration, fired it at his intended victim. But Rigaud remained unharmed, and, in the scuffle which ensued, the white assassin was disarmed and put to flight. The astonishment of the mulattoes soon gave way to tumult and indignation, and this produced a drawn battle, in which both whites and mulattoes, exasperated as they were to the utmost, fought man to man. The struggle continued fiercely until the whites were driven from the town, having lost one hundred and fifty of their number, and slain many of their opponents.

Tidings of this conspiracy flew rapidly in all directions; and such was the indignation of the mulattoes at this attack upon their chief, whose death had even been announced in several places as certain, that they seized upon all the whites within their reach; and their immediate massacre was only prevented by the arrival of intelligence that Rigaud was still alive. Such were the persecutions which the leader of the mulattoes, now in exile, had experienced in his own land. Napoleon kept him confined in the prison of the Temple first, and then at the castle of Joux, where Toussaint had ended his life.

During this time, St. Domingo was undergoing a great change. Leclerc had died, Rochambeau and his forces had been driven from the island, Dessalines had reigned and passed away, and Christophe was master of the north, and Petion of the south. These two generals were at war with each other, when they were both very much surprised at the arrival of Rigaud from France. He had escaped from his prison, made his way to England, and thence to the island by way of the United States. Petion, the president of the republic in the south, regarded Rigaud as a more formidable enemy than Christophe. The great mulatto general was welcomed with enthusiasm by his old adherents; they showed the most sincere respect and attachment for him, and he journeyed in triumph to Port au Prince. Though Petion disliked these demonstrations in favor of a rival, he dared not attempt to interfere, for he well knew that a single word from Rigaud could raise a revolt among the mulattoes. Petion, himself a mulatto, had served under the former in the first stages of the revolution. The people of Aux Cayes welcomed their chief to his home, and he drew around him all hearts, and in a short time Rigaud was in full possession of his ancient power. The government of Petion was divided to make room for the former chief, and, though the two leaders for a while flew to arms against each other, they, nevertheless, were driven to an alliance on account of the encroachments of Christophe.

After a reign that was fraught only with tumult to himself and followers, Rigaud abdicated his province, retired to his farm, and in a few weeks died. Thus ended the career of the most distinguished mulatto general of which St. Domingo could boast.

## FRANCES ELLEN WATKINS.

MISS WATKINS is a native of Baltimore, where she received her education. She has been before the public some years as an author and public lecturer. Her "Poems on Miscellaneous Subjects," published in a small volume, show a reflective mind and no ordinary culture. Her "Essay on Christianity" is a beautiful composition. Many of her poems are soul-stirring, and all are characterized by chaste language and much thought. The following is entitled

## THE SLAVE MOTHER.

Heard you that shriek? It rose
So wildly on the air,
It seemed as if a burdened heart
Was breaking in despair.

Saw you those hands so sadly clasped,
The bowed and feeble head,
The shuddering of that fragile form,
That look of grief and dread?

Saw you the sad, imploring eye?
Its every glance was pain,
As if a storm of agony
Were sweeping through the brain.

She is a mother pale with fear;
Her boy clings to her side,
And in her kirtle vainly tries
His trembling form to hide.

He is not hers, although she bore
For him a mother's pains;
He is not hers, although her blood
Is coursing through his veins.

He is not hers, for cruel hands
May rudely tear apart
The only wreath of household love
That binds her breaking heart.

His love has been a joyous light
That o'er her pathway smiled,
A fountain, gushing ever new,
Amid life's desert wild.

His lightest word has been a tone
Of music round her heart;
Their lives a streamlet blent in one--
O Father, must they part?

They tear him from her circling arms,
Her last and fond embrace;
O, never more may her sad eyes
Gaze on his mournful face.

No marvel, then, these bitter shrieks
Disturb the listening air;
She is a mother, and her heart
Is breaking in despair.

Miss Watkins's advice to her own sex on the selection of a husband should be appreciated by all.

Nay, do not blush! I only heard
You had a mind to marry;
I thought I'd speak a friendly word
So just one moment tarry.

Wed not a man whose merit lies
In things of outward show,
In raven hair or flashing eyes,
That please your fancy so.

But marry one who's good and kind,
And free from all pretence;
Who, if without a gifted mind,
At least has common sense.

Miss Watkins is about thirty years of age, of a fragile form, rather nervous, keen and witty in conversation, outspoken in her opinions, and yet appears in all the simplicity of a child.

# EX-PRESIDENT ROBERTS.

J. J. ROBERTS, ex-president of the Republic of Liberia, is a native of the Old Dominion, and emigrated to his adopted country about twenty-five years ago. In stature he is tall, slim, and has a commanding appearance, sharp features, pleasant countenance, and is what the ladies would call "good looking." Mr. Roberts has much the bearing of an "English gentleman." He has fine abilities, and his state papers will compare favorably with the public documents of any of the presidents of the United States. He is thoroughly devoted to the interest of the rising republic, and has visited Europe several times in her behalf.

The following extract from the inaugural address of President Roberts to the legislature of Liberia, in 1848, on the colonists taking the entire responsibility of the government, is eloquent and pointed:--

"It must afford the most heartfelt pleasure and satisfaction to every friend of Liberia, and real lover of liberty, to observe by what a fortunate train of circumstances and incidents the people of these colonies have arrived at absolute freedom and independence. When we look abroad and see by what slow and painful steps, marked with blood and ills of every kind, other states of the world have advanced to liberty and independence, we cannot but admire and praise that all-gracious Providence, who, by his unerring ways, has, with so few sufferings on our part, compared with other states, led us to this happy stage in our progress towards those great and important objects. That it is the will of Heaven that mankind should be free, is clearly evidenced by the wealth, vigor, virtue, and consequent happiness of all free states. But the idea that Providence will establish such governments as he shall deem most fit for his creatures, and will give them wealth, influence, and happiness without their efforts, is palpably absurd. God's moral government of the earth is always performed by the intervention of second causes. Therefore, fellow-citizens, while with pious gratitude we survey the frequent interpositions of Heaven in our behalf, we ought to remember, that as the disbelief of an overruling Providence is atheism, so an absolute confidence of having our government relieved from every embarrassment, and its citizens made respectable and happy by the immediate hand of God, without our own exertions, is the most culpable presumption. Nor have we any reason to expect, that he will miraculously make Liberia a paradise, and deliver us, in a moment of time, from all the ills and inconveniences consequent upon the peculiar circumstances under which we are placed, merely to convince us that he favors our cause and government.

"Sufficient indications of his will are always given, and those who will not then believe, neither would they believe though one should rise from the dead to inform them. Who can trace the progress of these colonies, and mark the incidents of the wars in which they have been engaged, without seeing evident tokens of providential favor. Let us, therefore, inflexibly persevere in exerting our most strenuous efforts in a humble and rational dependence on the great Governor of all the world, and we have the fairest prospects of surmounting all the difficulties which may be thrown in our way. That we may expect, and that we shall have, difficulties, sore difficulties, yet to contend against in our progress to maturity, is certain; and, as the political happiness or wretchedness of ourselves and our children, and of generations yet unborn, is in our hands,--nay, more, the redemption of Africa from the deep degradation, superstition, and idolatry in which she has so long been involved,--it becomes us to lay our shoulders to the wheel, and manfully resist every obstacle which may oppose our progress in the great work which lies before us."

Mr. Roberts, we believe, is extensively engaged in commerce and agriculture, and, though out of office, makes himself useful in the moral, social, and intellectual elevation of his brethren. No one is more respected, or stands higher, in Liberia than he.

## ALEXANDER CRUMMELL.

AMONG the many bright examples of the black man which we present, one of the foremost is Alexander Crummell. Blood unadulterated, a tall and manly figure, commanding in appearance, a full and musical voice, fluent in speech, a graduate of Cambridge University, England, a mind stored with the richness of English literature, competently acquainted with the classical authors of Greece and Rome, from the grave Thucydides to the rhapsodical Lycophron, gentlemanly in all his movements, language chaste and refined, Mr. Crummell may well be put forward as one of the best and most favorable representatives of his race. He is a clergyman of the Episcopal denomination, and deeply versed in theology. His sermons are always written, but he reads them as few persons can. In 1848 Mr. Crummell visited England, and delivered a well-conceived address before the Anti-Slavery Society in London, where his eloquence and splendid abilities were at once acknowledged and appreciated. The year before his departure for the old world, he delivered a "Eulogy on the Life and Character of Thomas Clarkson," from which we make the following extract, which is full of meaning and eloquence:--

"Let us not be unmindful of the prerogatives and obligations arising from the fact, that the exhibition of the greatest talent, and the development of the most enlarged philanthropy, in the nineteenth century, have been bestowed upon our race. The names of the great lights of the age,--statesmen, poets, and divines,--in all the great countries of Europe, and in this country too, are inseparably connected with the cause and destiny of the African race. This has been the theme whence most of them have reaped honor and immortality. This cause has produced the development of the most noble character of modern times--has given the world a Wilberforce and a Clarkson. Lowly and depressed as we have been, and as we now are, yet our interests and our welfare have agitated the chief countries of the world, and are now before all other questions, shaking this nation to its very centre. The providences of God have placed the negro race before Europe and America in the most commanding position. From the sight of us no nation, no statesman, no ecclesiastic, and no ecclesiastical institution, can escape. And by us and our cause the character and greatness of individuals and of nations in this day and generation of the world are to be decided, either for good or evil; and so, in all coming times, the memory and the fame of the chief actors now on the stage will be decided by their relation to our cause. The discoveries of science, the unfoldings of literature, the dazzlings of genius, all fade before the demands of this cause. This is the age of BROTHERHOOD AND HUMANITY, and the negro race is its most distinguished test and criterion.

"And for what are all these providences? For nothing? He who thinks so must be blinded--must be demented. In these facts are wound up a most distinct significance, and with them are connected most clear and emphatic obligations and responsibilities. The clear-minded and thoughtful colored men of America must mark the significance of these facts, and begin to feel their weight. For more than two centuries we have been working our way from the deep and dire degradation into which slavery had plunged us. We have made considerable headway. By the vigorous use of the opportunities of our partial freedom we have been enabled, with the divine blessing, to reach a position of respectability and character. We have pressed somewhat into the golden avenues of science, intelligence, and learning. We have made impressions there; and some few of our footprints have we left behind. The mild light of religion has illumined our pathway, and superstition and error have fled apace. The greatest paradoxes are evinced by us. Amid the decay of nations, a rekindled light starts up in us. Burdens under which others expire seem to have lost their influence upon us; and while they are 'driven to the wall,' destruction keeps far from us its blasting hand. We live in the region of death, yet seem hardly mortal. We cling to life in the midst of all reverses; and our nerveful grasp thereon cannot easily be relaxed. History reverses its mandates in our behalf: our dotage is in the past. 'Time writes not its wrinkles on our brow;' our juvenescence is in the future. All this, and the kindly nature which is acknowledgedly ours,--with gifts of freedom vouchsafed us by the Almighty in this land, in part, and in the West Indies; with the intellectual desire every where manifesting itself, and the exceeding interest exhibited for Africa by her own children, and by the Christian nations of the world, are indications from which we may not gather a trivial meaning, nor a narrow significance.

"The teaching of God in all these things is, undoubtedly, that ours is a great destiny, and that we should open our eyes to it. God is telling us all that, whereas the past has been dark, grim, and repulsive, the future shall be glorious; that the horrid traffic shall yet be entirely stopped; that the whips and brands, the shackles and fetters, of slavery shall be cast down to oblivion; that the shades of ignorance and superstition that have so long settled down upon the mind of Africa shall be dispelled; and that all her sons on her own broad continent, in the Western Isles, and in this Republic, shall yet stand erect beneath the heavens, 'with freedom chartered on their manly brows;' their bosoms swelling with its noblest raptures --treading the face of earth in the links of brotherhood and equality."

We have had a number of our public men to represent us in Europe within the past twenty-five years and none have done it more honorably or with better success to the character and cause of the black man, than Alexander Crummell. We met him there again and again, and followed in his track wherever he preached or spoke before public assemblies, and we know whereof we affirm. In 1852, we believe, he went to Liberia, where he now resides. At present he and his family are on a visit to "the States," partly for his health and partly for the purpose of promoting emigration to Africa. Mr. C. has recently published a valuable work on Africa, which is highly spoken of by the press; indeed, it may be regarded as the only finished account of our mother land. Devotedly attached to the interest of the colored man, and having the moral, social, and intellectual elevation of the natives of Africa at heart, we do not regret that he considers it his duty to labor in his father land. Warmly interested in the Republic, and so capable of filling the highest position that he can be called to, we shall not be surprised, some day, to hear that Alexander Crummell is president of Liberia.

## ALEXANDRE PETION.

THE ambitious and haughty mulattoes had long been dissatisfied with the obscure condition into which they had been thrown by the reign of Dessalines, and at the death of that ruler they determined to put forward their claim. Their great chief, Rigaud, was still in prison in France, where he had been placed by Napoleon. Christophe had succeeded to power at the close of the empire, and was at St. Marks when he heard that Alexandre Petion had been elected president of the Republic of Hayti, through the instrumentality of the mulattoes. Christophe at once began to prepare for war. Petion was a quadroon, the successor of Rigaud and Clervaux to the confidence of the mulattoes. He was a man of education and refined manners. He had been educated at the Military School of Paris, and had ever been characterized for his mildness of temper and the insinuating grace of his address. He was a skilful engineer, and at the time of his elevation to power he passed for the most scientific officer and the most erudite individual among the people of Hayti. Attached to the fortunes of Rigaud, he had acted as his lieutenant against Toussaint, and had accompanied him to France. Here he remained until the departure of the expedition under Leclerc, when he embarked in that disastrous enterprise, to employ his talents in again restoring his country to the dominion of France. Petion joined Dessalines, Christophe, and Clervaux, when they revolted and turned against the French, and aided in gaining the final independence of the island. Christophe, therefore, as soon as he heard that he had a rival in Petion, rallied his forces, and started for Port au Prince, to meet his enemy. The former was already in the field, and the two armies met; a battle ensued, and Petion, being defeated, and hotly pursued in his flight, found it necessary, in order to save his life, to exchange his uniform with a laborer, and to bury himself up to his neck in a marsh until his fierce pursuers had disappeared. Petion escaped, and reached his capital before the arrival of the troops under Christophe. The latter, after this signal success,pressed forward to Port au Prince, and laid siege to the town, in hope of an easy triumph over his rival. But Petion was in his appropriate sphere of action, and Christophe soon discovered that, in contending with an experienced engineer in a fortified town, success was of more difficult attainment than while encountering the same enemy in the open field, where his science could not be brought into action. Christophe could make no impression on the town, and feeling ill assured of the steadfastness of his own proper government at Cape François, he withdrew his forces from the investment of Port au Prince, resolved to establish in the north a separate government of his own, and to defer to some more favorable opportunity the attempt to subdue his rival at Port au Prince. In September, 1808, Petion commenced another campaign against Christophe, by sending an army to besiege Port de Paix, which it did; but after a while it was driven back to Port au Prince by the victorious legions of the president of the north. Christophe in turn attempted to take the Mole St. Nicholas from Lamarre, one of Petion's generals, but did not succeed. The struggle between the two presidents of Hayti had now continued three years, when a new competitor appeared in the field, by the arrival of Rigaud from France. This was an unexpected event, which awakened deep solicitude in the bosom of Petion, who could not avoid regarding that distinguished general as a more formidable rival than Christophe. He well knew the attachment of the people to the great mulatto chief, and he feared his superior talents. The enthusiasm with which Rigaud was received wherever he appeared, raised the jealousy of Petion to such a pitch, that he for a time forgot his black rival. Partisans flew to the standard of Rigaud, and a resort to arms seemed imminent between him and Petion. A meeting, however, was held by the two mulatto generals, at the bridge of Miragoane, where a treaty was signed, by which the south was to be governed by the former, and the west, and as much as could be wrested from Christophe, by the latter. But peace between these two was not destined to be of long duration. A war took place, and Rigaud's troops proved too much for Petion, and he was defeated with great loss, and his entire army almost annihilated. But the victorious general did not follow up his successes; and although he had gained a signal victory, he felt that much of his power over his followers was passing away. The death of Rigaud once more gave the field to Christophe and Petion, and they again commenced war upon each other. The latter was superior to the former in education, and in the refinement given him by a cultivated understanding and an extensive intercourse with European society; but he was greatly inferior to Christophe in boldness and decision of character. Petion was subtle, cautious, and desponding. He aspired to be the Washington, as Christophe was deemed the Bonaparte, of Hayti. By insinuating the doctrines of equality and republicanism, Petion succeeded in governing, with but ten thousand mulattoes, a population of more than two hundred thousand blacks. Assuming no pretensions to personal or official dignity, and totally rejecting all the ceremonial of a court, it was Petion's ambition to maintain the exterior of a plain republican magistrate. Clad in the white linen undress of the country, and with a Madras handkerchief tied about his head, he mixed freely and promiscuously with his fellow-citizens, or seated himself in the piazza of the government house, accessible to all. He professed to hold himself at the disposal of the people, and to be ready at any moment to submit to their will, whether it was to guide the power of the state, or yield his head to the executioner.

A republican officer one day called on Petion at the government house, and while they were alone, the former drew out a pistol and fired at the president, without injuring him, however; the latter immediately seized his visitor, disarmed him, and when the guard rushed in, he found the president and the officer walking the room locked in each other's arms. This man was ever after the warm friend of Petion. At the downfall of Napoleon, and the elevation of Louis XVIII., another effort was made to regain possession of the island by France. But the latter did not resort to arms. Having no confidence in the French, and fearing a warlike demonstration, both Petion and Christophe prepared for defence. Petion had long been despondent for the permanence of the republic, and this feeling had by degrees grown into a settled despair; and amidst these perplexities and embarrassments he fell sick, in the month of March, 1818, and after an illness which continued only eight days, he died, and was succeeded by General Boyer.

The administration of Petion was mild, and he did all that he could for the elevation of the people whom he ruled. He was the patron of education and the arts, and scientific men, for years after his death, spoke his name with reverence. He was highly respected by the representatives of foreign powers, and strangers visiting his republic always mentioned his name in connection with the best cultivated and most gentlemanly of the people of Hayti. Lightly lie the earth on the bones of Petion, and let every cloud pass away from his memory.

# MARTIN R. DELANY, M.D.

DR. DELANY has long been before the public. His first appearance we believe, was in connection with The Mystery, a weekly newspaper published at Pittsburg, and of which he was editor. His journal was faithful in its advocacy of the rights of man, and had the reputation of being a well-conducted sheet. The doctor afterwards was associated with Frederick Douglass in the editorial management of his paper at Rochester, N. Y. From the latter place he removed to Canada, and has since resided in Chatham, where he is looked upon as one of its leading citizens.

Dr. M. R. Delany, though regarded as a man high in his profession, is better and more widely known as a traveller, discoverer, and lecturer. His association with Professor Campbell in the "Niger Valley Exploring Expedition" has brought the doctor very prominently before the world, and especially that portion of it which takes an interest in the civilization of Africa. The official report of that expedition shows that he did not visit that country with his eyes shut. His observations and suggestions about the climate, soil, diseases, and natural productions of Africa, are interesting, and give evidence that the doctor was in earnest. The published report, of which he is the author, will repay, a perusal.

On his return home, Dr. Delany spent some time in England, and lectured in the British metropolis and the provincial cities, with considerable success, on Africa and its resources. As a member of the International Statistical Congress, he acquitted himself with credit to his position and honor to his race. The foolish manner in which the Hon. Mr. Dallas, our Minister to the court of St. James, acted on meeting Dr. Delany in that august assembly, and the criticisms of the press of Europe and America, will not soon be forgotten.

He is short, compactly built, has a quick, wiry walk, and is decided and energetic in conversation, unadulterated in race, and proud of his complexion. Though somewhat violent in his gestures, and paying but little regard to the strict rules of oratory, Dr. Delany is, nevertheless, an interesting, eloquent speaker. Devotedly attached to his fatherland, he goes for a "Negro Nationality." Whatever he undertakes, he executes it with all the powers that God has given him; and what would appear as an obstacle in the way of other men, would be brushed aside by Martin R. Delany.

# ROBERT SMALL.

AT the breaking out of the rebellion, Robert Small was a slave in Charleston, S. C. He stood amid a group of his fellow-slaves, as the soldiers were getting ready to make the assault upon Fort Sumter, and he said to his associates, "This, boys, is the dawn of freedom for our race." Robert, at this time, was employed as pilot on board the steamboat "Planter," owned at Charleston, and then lying at her dock. The following day, the steamer commenced undergoing alterations necessary to fit her for a gunboat. Robert, when within hearing of the whites, was loud in his talk of what "we'll do with the Yankees, when this boat is ready for sea." The Planter was soon transmogrified into a rebel man-of-war, to be used in and about the rivers and bays near Charleston, and Robert Small was her acknowledged pilot. One of Robert's brothers was second engineer, and a cousin to him was the second mate; the remainder of the crew were all slaves, except the white officers. It was the custom of the captain, chief mate, and chief engineer to spend the night with their families in the city, when the steamer was in port, the vessel being left in charge of Robert. The following is the account of the capture of the boat by her black crew, as given by the Port Royal correspondent of the New York Commercial Advertiser:--

"The steamer Planter, which was run away from the rebels by her pilot, Robert Small, is a new tug boat employed about Charleston harbor, which was seized by the Confederate government and converted into a gunboat, mounting a rifled gun forward and a siege gun aft. She has been in the habit of running out to sea to reconnoitre, and was, therefore, no unusual appearance near the forts guarding the entrance. Small, the helmsman and pilot, conceived the idea of running away, and plotted with several friends, slaves like him, to take them off.

"On the evening of May 11, her officers left the ship, then at the wharf in Charleston, and went to their homes. Small then took the firemen and assistant engineers, all of whom were slaves, in his confidence, had the fires banked up, and every thing made ready to start by daylight.

"At quarter to four on Saturday morning, the lines which fastened the vessel to the dock were cast off, and the ship quietly glided into the stream. Here the harbor guard hailed the vessel, but Small promptly gave the countersign, and was allowed to pass.

"The vessel now called at a dock a distance below, where the families of the crew came on board.

"When off Fort Sumter, the sentry on the ramparts hailed the boat, and Small sounded the countersign with the whistle--three shrill sounds and one hissing sound. The vessel being known to the officers of the day, no objection was raised, the sentry only singing out, 'Blow the d--d Yankees to hell, or bring one of them in.' 'Ay, ay,' was the answer, and every possible effort was made to get below.

"Hardly was the vessel out of range, when Small ran up a white flag, and went to the United States fleet, where he surrendered the vessel. She had on board seven heavy guns for Fort Ripley, a fort now building in Charleston harbor, which were to be taken thither the next morning.

"Small, with the crew and their families,--sixteen persons,--were sent to the flagship at Port Royal, and an officer placed on board the Planter, who took her also to Commodore Dupont's vessel. Small is a middle-aged negro, and his features betray nothing of the firmness of character he displayed. He is said to be one of the most skilful pilots of Charleston, and to have a thorough knowledge of all the ports and inlets on the coast of South Carolina.'

We give below the official account of the taking and surrender of the boat to the naval authorities.

U. S. STEAMSHIP AUGUSTA, OFF CHARLESTON, May 13, 1862.

Sir: I have the honor to inform you that the rebel armed steamer Planter was brought out to us this morning from Charleston by eight contrabands, and delivered up to the squadron. Five colored women and three children are also on board. She carried one 32-pounder and one 24-pounder howitzer, and has also on board four large guns, which she was engaged in transporting. I send her to Port Royal at once, in order to take advantage of the present good weather. I send Charleston papers of the 12th, and the very intelligent contraband who was in charge will give you the information which he has brought off. I have the honor to request that you will send back, as soon as convenient, the officer and crew sent on board.

Commander Dupont, in forwarding the despatch, says, in relation to the steamer Planter,-
-

She was the armed despatch and transportation steamer attached to the engineer department at Charleston, under Brigadier General Ripley, whose bark, a short time since, was brought to the blockading fleet by several contrabands. The bringing out of this steamer, under all the circumstances, would have done credit to any one. At four in the morning, in the absence of the captain, who was on shore, she left her wharf close to the government office and headquarters, with the Palmetto and "Confederate" flags flying, and passed the successive forts, saluting, as usual, by blowing the steam whistle. After getting beyond the range of the last gun, they hauled down the rebel flags, and hoisted a white one. The Onward was the inside ship of the blockading squadron in the main channel, and was preparing to fire when her commander made out the white flag. The armament of the steamer is a 32-pounder, or pivot, and a fine 24-pound howitzer. She has besides, on her deck, four other guns, one seven inch rifled, which were to be taken, on the morning of the escape, to the new fort on the middle ground. One of the four belonged to Fort Sumter, and had been struck, in the rebel attack, on the muzzle. Robert Small, the intelligent slave, and pilot of the boat, who performed this bold feat so skilfully, informed me of this fact, presuming it would be a matter of interest to us to have possession of this gun. This man, Robert Small, is superior to any who have come into our lines, intelligent as many of them have been. His information has been most interesting, and portions of it of the utmost importance. The steamer is quite a valuable acquisition to the squadron by her good machinery and very light draught. The officer in charge brought her through St. Helena Sound, and by the inland passage down Beaufort River, arriving here at ten last night. On board the steamer, when she left Charleston, were eight men, five women, and three children. I shall continue to employ Small as pilot on board the Planter, for inland waters, with which he appears to be very familiar.

I do not know whether, in the view of the government, the vessel will be considered a prize; but if so, I respectfully submit to the Department the claims of the man Small and his associates.

Very respectfully, your obedient servant,

S. F. DUPONT,

Flag Officer, Commanding, &c.

A bill was at once introduced in Congress to consider the Planter a prize, and to award the prize-money to her crew. The New York Tribune had the following editorial on the subject:--

"The House of Representatives at Washington, it is to be hoped, will be more just to their own sense of right, and to their more generous impulses, than to put aside again the Senate bill giving the prize-money they have so well earned to the pilot and crew of the steamer Planter. Neither House would have done an act unworthy of their dignity had they promptly passed a vote of thanks to Robert Small and his fellows for the cool courage with which they planned and executed their escape from rebel bondage, and the unswerving loyalty which prompted them, at the same time, to bring away such spoils from the enemy as would make a welcome addition to the blockading squadron.

"If we must still remember with humiliation that the Confederate flag yet waves where our national colors were first struck, we should be all the more prompt to recognize the merit that has put into our possession the first trophy from Fort Sumter. And the country should feel doubly humbled if there is not magnanimity enough to acknowledge a gallant action, because it was the head of a black man that conceived, and the hand of a black man that executed it. It would better, indeed, become us to remember that no small share of the naval glory of the war belongs to the race which we have forbidden to fight for us; that one negro has recaptured a vessel from a southern privateer, and another has brought away from under the very guns of the enemy, where no fleet of ours has yet dared to venture, a prize whose possession a commodore thinks worthy to be announced in a special despatch."

The bill was taken up and passed, and the brave Small and his companions received justice at the hands of the government.

# FREDERICK DOUGLASS.

THE career of the distinguished individual whose name heads this page is more widely known than that of any other living colored man, except, perhaps, Alexandre Dumas. The narrative of his life, published in 1845, gave a new impetus to the black man's literature. All other stories of fugitive slaves faded away before the beautifully written, highly descriptive,and thrilling memoir of Frederick Douglass. Other narratives had only brought before the public a few heart-rending scenes connected with the person described. But Mr. Douglass, in his book, brought not only his old master's farm and its occupants before the reader, but the entire country around him, including Baltimore and its ship yard. The manner in which he obtained his education, and especially his learning to write, has been read and re-read by thousands in both hemispheres. His escape from slavery is too well understood to need a recapitulation here. He took up his residence in New Bedford, where he still continued the assiduous student--mastering the different branches of education which the accursed institution had deprived him of in early life.

His advent as a lecturer was a remarkable one. White men and black men had talked against slavery, but none had ever spoken like Frederick Douglass. Throughout the north the newspapers were filled with the sayings of the "eloquent fugitive." He often travelled with others, but they were all lost sight of in the eagerness to hear Douglass. His travelling companions would sometimes get angry, and would speak first at the meetings; then they would take the last turn; but it was all the same--the fugitive's impression was the one left upon the mind. He made more persons angry, and pleased more, than any other man. He was praised, and he was censured. He made them laugh, he made them weep, and he made them swear. His "Slaveholder's Sermon" was always a trump card. He awakened an interest in the hearts of thousands who before were dead to the slave and his condition. Many kept away from his lectures, fearing lest they should be converted against their will. Young men and women, in those days of pro-slavery hatred, would return to their fathers' roofs filled with admiration for the "runaway slave," and would be rebuked by hearing the old ones grumble out, "You'd better stay at home and study your lessons, and not be running after the nigger meetings."

In 1841, he was induced to accept an agency as a lecturer for the Anti-slavery Society, and at once became one of the most valuable of its advocates. He visited England in 1845. There he was kindly received, and heartily welcomed; and after going through the length and breadth of the land, and addressing public meetings out of number on behalf of his countrymen in chains, with a power of eloquence which captivated his auditors, and brought the cause which he pleaded home to their hearts, he returned home and commenced the publication of the North Star, a weekly newspaper devoted to the advocacy of the cause of freedom.

Mr. Douglass is tall and well made. His vast and fully-developed forehead shows at once that he is a superior man intellectually. He is polished in his language, and gentlemanly in his manners. His voice is full and sonorous. His attitude is dignified, and his gesticulation is full of noble simplicity. He is a man of lofty reason; natural, and without pretension; always master of himself; brilliant in the art of exposing and abstracting. Few persons can handle a subject, with which they are familiar, better than he. There is a kind of eloquence issuing from the depth of the soul as from a spring, rolling along its copious floods, sweeping all before it, overwhelming by its very force, carrying, upsetting, ingulfing its adversaries, and more dazzling and more thundering than the bolt which leaps from crag to crag. This is the eloquence of Frederick Douglass. One of the best mimics of the age, and possessing great dramatic powers, had he taken up the sock and buskin, instead of becoming a lecturer, he would have made as fine a Coriolanus as ever trod the stage.

In his splendidly conceived comparison of Mr. Douglass to S. R. Ward, written for the "Autographs for Freedom," Professor William J. Wilson says of the former, "In his very look, his gesture, his whole manner, there is so much of genuine, earnest eloquence, that they leave no time for reflection. Now you are reminded of one rushing down some fearful steep, bidding you follow; now on some delightful stream, still beckoning you onward. In either case, no matter what your prepossessions or oppositions, you, for the moment at least, forget the justness or unjustness of his cause, and obey the summons, and loath, if at all, you return to your former post. Not always, however, is he successful in retaining you. Giddy as you may be with the descent you have made, delighted as you are with the pleasure afforded, with the Elysium to which he has wafted you, you return too often dissatisfied with his and your own impetuosity and want of firmness. You feel that you had only a dream, a pastime,--not a reality.

"This great power of momentary captivation consists in his eloquence of manners, his just appreciation of words. In listening to him, your whole soul is fired, every nerve strung, every passion inflated, and every faculty you possess ready to perform at a moment's bidding. You stop not to ask why or wherefore. 'Tis a unison of mighty yet harmonious sounds that play upon your imagination; and you give yourself up, for a time, to their irresistible charm. At last, the cataract which roared around you is hushed, the tornado is passed, and you find yourself sitting upon a bank, (at whose base roll but tranquil waters,) quietly asking yourself why, amid such a display of power, no greater effect had really been produced. After all, it must be admitted there is a power in Mr. Douglass rarely to be found in any other man."

As a speaker, Frederick Douglass has had more imitators than almost any other American, save, perhaps, Wendell Phillips. Unlike most great speakers, he is a superior writer also. Some of his articles, in point of ability, will rank with any thing ever written for the American press. He has taken lessons from the best of teachers, amid the homeliest realities of life; hence the perpetual freshness of his delineations, which are never over-colored, never strained, never aiming at difficult or impossible effects, but which always read like living transcripts of experience. The following, from his pen, on "What shall be done with the slaves, if emancipated?" is characteristic of his style.

"What shall be done with the four million slaves, if they are emancipated? This question has been answered, and can be answered in many ways. Primarily, it is a question less for man than for God-- less for human intellect than for the laws of nature to solve. It assumes that nature has erred; that the law of liberty is a mistake; that freedom, though a natural want of the human soul, can only be enjoyed at the expense of human welfare, and that men are better off in slavery than they would or could be in freedom; that slavery is the natural order of human relations, and that liberty is an experiment. What shall be done with them?

"Our answer is, Do nothing with them; mind your business, and let them mind theirs. Your doing with them is their greatest misfortune. They have been undone by your doings, and all they now ask, and really have need of at your hands, is just to let them alone. They suffer by every interference, and succeed best by being let alone. The negro should have been let alone in Africa--let alone when the pirates and robbers offered him for sale in our Christian slave markets (more cruel and inhuman than the Mohammedan slave markets)--let alone by courts, judges, politicians, legislators, and slave-drivers--let alone altogether, and assured that they were thus to be let alone forever, and that they must now make their own way in the world, just the same as any and every other variety of the human family. As colored men, we only ask to be allowed to do with ourselves, subject only to the same great laws for the welfare of human society which apply to other men--Jews, Gentiles, Barbarian, Scythian. Let us stand upon our own legs, work with our own hands, and eat bread in the sweat of our own brows. When you, our white fellow-countrymen, have attempted to do any thing for us, it has generally been to deprive us of some right, power, or privilege, which you yourselves would die before you would submit to have taken from you. When the planters of the West Indies used to attempt to puzzle the pure-minded Wilberforce with the question,'How shall we get rid of slavery?' his simple answer was, 'Quit stealing.' In like manner we answer those who are perpetually puzzling their brains with questions as to what shall be done with the negro, 'Let him alone, and mind your own business.' If you see him ploughing in the open field, levelling the forest, at work with a spade, a rake, a hoe, a pickaxe, or a bill--let him alone; he has a right to work. If you see him on his way to school, with spelling-book, geography, and arithmetic in his hands--let him alone. Don't shut the door in his face, nor bolt your gates against him; he has a right to learn--let him alone. Don't pass laws to degrade him. If he has a ballot in his hand, and is on his way to the ballot-box to deposit his vote for the man who, he thinks, will most justly and wisely administer the government which has the power of life and death over him, as well as others-- let him ALONE; his right of choice as much deserves respect and protection as your own. If you see him on his way to church, exercising religious liberty in accordance with this or that religious persuasion--let him alone. Don't meddle with him, nor trouble yourselves with any questions as to what shall be done with him.

"What shall be done with the negro, if emancipated? Deal justly with him. He is a human being, capable of judging between good and evil, right and wrong, liberty and slavery, and is as much a subject of law as any other man; therefore, deal justly with him. He is, like other men, sensible of the motives of reward and punishment. Give him wages for his work, and let hunger pinch him if he don't work. He knows the difference between fulness and famine, plenty and scarcity. "But will he work?" Why should he not? He is used to it, and is not afraid of it. His hands are already hardened by toil, and he has no dreams of ever getting a living by any other means than by hard work. "But would you turn them all loose?" Certainly! We are no better than our Creator. He has turned them loose, and why should not we? "But would you let them all stay here?" Why not? What better is here than there? Will they occupy more room as freemen than as slaves? Is the presence of a black freeman less agreeable than that of a black slave? Is an object of your injustice and cruelty a more ungrateful sight than one of your justice and benevolence? You have borne the one more than two hundred years--can't you bear the other long enough to try the experiment?

# CHARLES L. REASON.

PROFESSOR C. L. REASON has for many years been connected with the educational institutions of New York and Philadelphia. In 1849, he was called to the professorship of Mathematics and Belles Lettres in New York Central College. This situation he held during his own pleasure, with honor to himself and benefit to the students. A man of fine education, superior intelligence, gentlemanly in every sense of the term, of excellent discrimination, one of the best of students, Professor Reason holds a power over those under him seldom attained by men of his profession.

Were I a sculptor, and looking for a model of a perfect man in personal appearance, my selection would be Charles L. Reason. As a writer of both prose and poetry he need not be ashamed of his ability. Extremely diffident, be seldom furnishes any thing for the public eye. In a well-written essay on the propriety of establishing an industrial college, and the probable influence of the free colored people upon the emancipated blacks, he says, "Whenever emancipation shall take place, immediate though it be, the subjects of it, like many who now make up the so-called free population, will be, in what geologists call, the 'transition state.' The prejudice now felt against them for bearing on their persons the brand of slaves, cannot die out immediately. Severe trials will still be their portion: the curse of a 'taunted race,' must be expiated by almost miraculous proofs of advancement; and some of these miracles must be antecedent to the great day of jubilee. To fight the battle upon the bare ground of abstract principles will fail to give us complete victory. The subterfuges of pro-slavery selfishness must now be dragged to light, and the last weak argument, that the negro can never contribute any thing to advance the national character, 'nailed to the counter as base coin.' To the conquering of the difficulties heaped up in the path of his industry, the free colored man of the north has pledged himself. Already he sees, springing into growth, from out his foster work-school, intelligent young laborers, competent to enrich the world with necessary products; industrious citizens, contributing their proportion to aid on the advancing civilization of the country; self-providing artisans, vindicating their people from the never-ceasing charge of fitness for servile positions." In the "Autographs for Freedom," from which the above extract is taken, Professor Reason has a beautiful poem, entitled "Hope and Confidence," which, in point of originality and nicety of composition, will give it a place with the best productions of Wordsworth.

A poem signifies design, method, harmony, and therefore consistency of parts. A man may be gifted with the most vividly ideal nature; he may shoot from his brain some blazing poetic thought or imagery, which may arouse wonder and admiration, as a comet does; and yet he may have no constructiveness, without which the materials of poetry are only so many glittering fractions. A poem call never be tested by its length or brevity, but by the adaptation of its parts. A complete poem is the architecture of thought and language. It requires artistic skill to chisel rough blocks of marble into as many individual forms of beauty; but not only skill, but genius, is needed to arrange and harmonize those forms into the completeness of a Parthenon. A grave popular error, and one destructive of personal usefulness, and obstructive to literary progress, is the free-and-easy belief that because a man has the faculty of investing common things with uncommon ideas, therefore he can write a poem.

The idea of poetry is to give pleasurable emotions, and the world listens to a poet's voice as it listens to the singing of a summer bird; that which is the most suggestive of freedom and eloquence being the most admired. Professor Reason has both the genius and the artistic skill. We regret that we are able to give only the last two verses of "Hope and Confidence."

> "There's nothing so lovely and bright below,
> As the shapes of the purified mind;
> Nought surer to which the weak heart can grow,
> On which it can rest as it onward doth go,
> Than that Truth which its own tendrils bind.
>
> "Yes, Truth opes within a pure sun-tide of bliss,
> And shows in its ever calm flood
> A transcript of regions where no darkness is,
> Where Hope its conceptions may realize,
> And Confidence sleep in the good."

## CHARLOTTE L. FORTEN.

IN the autumn of 1854, a young colored lady of seventeen summers, unable to obtain admission into the schools of her native city (Philadelphia) on account of her complexion, removed to Salem, Massachusetts, where she at once entered the Higginson Grammar School. Here she soon secured the respect and esteem of the teachers and her fellow-pupils. Near the end of the last term, the principal of the establishment invited the scholars to write a poem each, to be sung at the last day's examination, and at the same time expressing the desire that the authors should conceal their names. As might have been expected, this drew out all the poetical genius of the young aspirants. Fifty or more manuscripts were sent in, and one selected, printed on a neat sheet, and circulated through the vast audience who were present. The following is the piece:--

# A PARTING HYMN.

When Winter's royal robes of white
From hill and vale are gone,
And the glad voices of the spring
Upon the air are borne,
Friends, who have met with us before,
within these walls shall meet no more.

Forth to a noble work they go:
O, may their hearts keep pure,
And hopeful zeal and strength be theirs
To labor and endure,
That they an earnest faith may prove
By words of truth and deeds of love.

May those, whose holy task it is
To guide impulsive youth,
Fail not to cherish in their souls
A reverence for truth;
For teachings which the lips impart
Must have their source within the heart.

May all who suffer share their love--
The poor and the oppressed;
So shall the blessing of our God
Upon their labors rest.
And may we meet again where all
Are blest and freed from every thrall.

The announcement that the successful competitor would be called out at the close of the singing, created no little sensation amongst the visitors, to say nothing of the pupils.

The principal of the school, after all parties had taken their seats, mounted the platform, and said, "Ladies and gentlemen, the beautiful hymn just sung is the composition of one of the students of this school, but who the talented person is I am unaware. Will the author step forward?" A moment's silence, and every eye was turned in the direction of the principal, who, seeing no one stir, looked around with a degree of amazement. Again he repeated, "Will the author of the hymn step forward?" A movement now among the female pupils showed that the last call had been successful. The buzzing and whispering throughout the large hall indicated the intense interest felt by all. "Sit down; keep your seats," exclaimed the principal, as the crowd rose to their feet, or bent forward to catch a glimpse of the young lady, who had now reached the front of the platform. Thunders of applause greeted the announcement that the distinguished authoress then before them was Miss Charlotte L. Forten. Her finely-chiselled features, well-developed forehead, countenance beaming with intelligence, and her dark complexion, showing her identity with an oppressed and injured race, all conspired to make the scene an exciting one. The audience was made up in part of some of the most aristocratic people in one of the most aristocratic towns in America. The impression left upon their minds was great in behalf of the race thus so nobly represented by the granddaughter of the noble-hearted, brave, generous, and venerable James Forten,whose whole life was a vindication of the character of his race.

"'Tis the mind that makes the body rich;
And as the sun breaks through the darkest clouds,

So honor peereth in the meanest habit."

For several days after the close of the school, the name of Charlotte L. Forten was mentioned in all the private circles of Salem; and to imitate her was the highest aspiration of the fairest daughters of that wealthy and influential city. Miss Forten afterwards entered the State Normal School, where, in the language of the Salem Register, "she graduated with decided eclat." She was then appointed by the school committee to be a teacher in the Epes Grammar School, where she "was graciously received," says the same journal, "by parents of the district, and soon endeared herself to the pupils under her charge." These pupils were all white. Aside from having a finished education, Miss Forten possesses genius of a high order. An excellent student and a lover of books, she has a finely-cultivated mind, well stored with incidents drawn from the classics. She evinces talent, as a writer, for both prose and poetry. The following extracts from her "Glimpses of New England," published in the National Anti-Slavery Standard, are characteristic of her prose. "The Old Witch House," at Salem, is thus described:--

"This street has also some interesting associations. It contains a very great attraction for all lovers of the olden time. This is an ancient, dingy, yellow frame house, known as "The Old Witch House." Our readers must know that Salem was, two hundred years ago, the headquarters of the witches. And this is the veritable old Court House where the so-called witches were tried and condemned. It is wonderful with what force this singular delusion possessed the minds, not only of the poor and ignorant, but of the wisest and gravest of the magistrates appointed by his majesty's government.

"Those were dark days for Salem. Woe to the housewife or the household over whose door latch the protecting horseshoe was not carefully placed; and far greater woe to the unlucky dame who chanced to be suspected of such fanciful freaks as riding through the air on a broomstick, or muttering mystic incantations wherewith to undo her innocent neighbors. Hers was a summary and terrible punishment. Well, it is very pleasant to think how times have changed, and to say with Whittier,--

'Our witches are no longer old
And wrinkled beldams, Satan-sold,
But young, and gay, and laughing creatures,
With the heart's sunshine on their features.'

Troops of such witches now pass the old house every day. I grieve to say that the 'Old Witch House' has recently been defaced and desecrated by the erection of an apothecary's shop in front of one of its wings. People say that the new shop is very handsome; but to a few of us, lovers of antiquity, it seems a profanation, and we can see no beauty in it."

The hills in the vicinity of Salem are beautifully pictured. "The pure, bracing air, the open sky," and the sheet of water in the distance, are all brought in with their lights and shades. Along with the brilliancy of style and warmth of imagination which characterize her writings, we find here and there gravity of thought and earnestness of purpose, befitting her literary taste. Of Marblehead Beach she writes,--

"The beach, which is at some distance from the town, is delightful. It was here that I first saw the sea, and stood 'entranced in silent awe,' gazing upon the waves as they marched, in one mass of the richest green, to the shore, then suddenly broke into foam, white and beautiful as the winter snow. I remember one pleasant afternoon which I spent with a friend, gathering shells and seaweed on the beach, or sitting on the rocks, listening, to the wild music of the waves, and watching the clouds of spray as they sprang high up in the air, then fell again in snowy wreaths at our feet. We lingered there until the sun had sunk into his ocean bed. On our homeward walk we passed Forest River, a winding, picturesque little stream, dotted with rocky islands. Over the river, and along our quiet way, the moon shed her soft and silvery light. And as we approached Salem, the lights, gleaming from every window of the large factory, gave us a cheerful welcome."

She "looks on nature with a poet's eye." The visit to Lynn is thus given:--

"Its chief attraction to me was 'High Rock,' on whose summit the pretty little dwelling of the Hutchinsons is perched like an eagle's eyrie. In the distance this rock looks so high and steep that one marvels how a house could ever have been built upon it. At its foot there once lived a famous fortune-teller of the olden time--'Moll Pitcher.' She at first resided in Salem, but afterwards removed to Lynn, where her fame spread over the adjoining country far and near. Whittier has made her the subject of a poem, which every one should read, not only for its account of the fortune-teller, but for its beautiful descriptions of the scenery around Lynn, especially of the bold Promontory of Nahant, whose fine beach, invigorating sea air, and, more than all, its grand, rugged old rocks,--the grandest I have ever seen,--washed by the waves of old Ocean, make it the most delightful of summer resorts."

The gifts of nature are of no rank or color; they come unbidden and unsought: as the wind awakes the chords of the Æolian harp, so the spirit breathes upon the soul, and brings to life all the melody of its being. The following poem recalls to recollection some of the beautiful yet solemn strains of Miss Landon, the gifted "L. E. L.," whose untimely death at Cape Coast Castle, some years since, carried sorrow to so many English hearts:--

## THE ANGEL'S VISIT.

'Twas on a glorious summer eve,--
A lovely eve in June,--
Serenely from her home above
Looked down the gentle moon;
And lovingly she smiled on me,
And softly soothed the pain--
The aching, heavy pain that lay
Upon my heart and brain.

And gently 'mid the murmuring leaves,
Scarce by its light wings stirred,
Like spirit voices soft and clear,
The night wind's song was heard;
In strains of music sweet and low
It sang to me of peace;

It bade my weary, troubled soul
Her sad complainings cease.

For bitter thoughts had filled my breast,
And sad, and sick at heart,
I longed to lay me down and rest,
From all the world apart.
"Outcast, oppressed on earth," I cried,
"O Father, take me home;
O take me to that peaceful land
Beyond the moon-lit dome.

"On such a night as this," methought,
"Angelic forms are near;
In beauty unrevealed to us
They hover in the air.
O mother, loved and lost," I cried,
"Methinks thou'rt near me now;

Methinks I feel thy cooling touch
Upon my burning brow.

"O, guide and soothe thy sorrowing child;
And if 'tis not His will
That thou shouldst take me home with thee,
Protect and bless me still;
For dark and drear had been my life
Without thy tender smile,
Without a mother's loving care,
Each sorrow to beguile."

I ceased: then o'er my senses stole
A soothing, dreamy spell,
And gently to my ear were borne
The tones I loved so well;

A sudden flood of rosy light
Filled all the dusky wood,
And, clad in shining robes of white,
My angel mother stood.

She gently drew me to her side,
She pressed her lips to mine,
And softly said, "Grieve not, my child;
A mother's love is thine.
I know the cruel wrongs that crush
The young and ardent heart;
But falter not; keep bravely on,
And nobly bear thy part.

"For thee a brighter day's in store;
And every earnest soul
That presses on, with purpose high,
Shall gain the wished-for goal.
And thou, beloved, faint not beneath
The weary weight of care;
Daily before our Father's throne
I breathe for thee a prayer.

"I pray that pure and holy thoughts
May bless and guard thy way;
A noble and unselfish life
For thee, my child, I pray."
She paused, and fondly bent on me
One lingering look of love,
Then softly said,--and passed away,--
"Farewell! we'll meet above."

I woke, and still the silver moon
In quiet beauty shone;

And still I heard amid the leaves
The night wind's murmuring tone;
But from my heart the weary pain
Forevermore had flown;
I knew a mother's prayer for me
Was breathed before the throne.

Nothing can be more touching than Miss Forten's illusion to her sainted mother. In some of her other poems she is more light and airy, and her muse delights occasionally to catch the sunshine on its aspiring wings. Miss Forten is still young, yet on the sunny side of twenty-five, and has a splendid future before her. Those who know her best consider her on the road to fame. Were she white, America would recognize her as one of its brightest gems.

## WILLIAM H. SIMPSON.

IT is a compliment to a picture to say that it produces the impression of the actual scene. Taste has, frequently, for its object works of art. Nature, many suppose, may be studied with propriety, but art they reject as entirely superficial. But what is the fact? In the highest sense, art is the child of nature, and is most admired when it preserves the likeness of its parent. In Venice, the paintings of Titian, and of the Venetian artists generally, exact from the traveller a yet higher tribute, for the hues and forms around him constantly remind him of their works. Many of the citizens of Boston are often called to mention the names of their absent or departed friends, by looking upon their features, as transferred to canvas by the pencil and brush of William H. Simpson, the young colored artist. He has evidently taken Titian, Murillo, and Raphael for his masters. The Venetian painters were diligent students of the nature that was around them. The subject of our sketch seems to have imbibed their energy, as well as learned to copy the noble example they left behind. The history of painters, as well as poets, is written in their works. The best life of Goldsmith is to be found in his poem of "The Traveller" and his novel of "The Vicar of Wakefield." No one views the beautiful portrait of Charles Kemble, in the National Gallery in London, in the character of Hamlet, without thinking of Sir Joshua Reynolds, who executed it. The organ of color is prominent in the cranium of Mr. Simpson, and it is well developed. His portraits are admired for their life-like appearance, as well as for the fine delineation which characterizes them all. It is very easy to transcribe the emotions which paintings awaken, but it is no easy matter to say why a picture is so painted as that it must awaken certain emotions. Many persons feel art, some understand it, but few both feel and understand it. Mr. Simpson is rich in depth of feeling and spiritual beauty. His portrait of John T. Hilton, which was presented to the Masonic Lodge a few months since, is a splendid piece of art. The longer you look on the features, the more the picture looks like real life. The taste displayed in the coloring of the regalia, and the admirable perspective of each badge of honor, shows great skill. No higher praise is needed than to say that a gentleman of Boston, distinguished for his good judgment in the picture gallery, wishing to secure a likeness of Hon. Charles Sumner, induced the senator to sit for Mr. Simpson for the portrait; and in this instance the artist has been signally successful.

His likenesses have been so correct, that he has often been employed to paint whole families, where only one had been bargained for in the commencement. He is considered unapproachable in taking juvenile faces. Mr. Simpson does not aspire to any thing in his art beyond portrait painting. Nevertheless, a beautiful fancy sketch, hanging in his studio, representing summer, exhibits marked ability and consummate genius. The wreath upon the head, with different kinds of grain interwoven, and the nicety of coloring in each particular kind, causes those who view it to regard him as master of his profession. Portraits of his execution are scattered over most of the Northern States and the Canadas. Some have gone to Liberia , Hayti, and California.

Mr. Simpson is a native of Buffalo, New York, where he received a liberal education. But even in school, his early inclination to draw likenesses materially interfered with his studies.

The propensity to use his slate and pencil in scratching down his schoolmates, instead of doing his sums in arithmetic, often gained him severe punishment. After leaving school, he was employed as errand boy by Matthew Wilson, Esq., the distinguished artist, who soon discovered young Simpson's genius, and took him as an apprentice. In 1854, they removed to Boston, where Mr. Simpson labored diligently to acquire a thorough knowledge of the profession. Mr. Wilson stated to the writer, that he never had a man who was more attentive or more trustworthy than William H. Simpson. The colored artist has been working in his own studio nearly three years, and has his share of public patronage. Of course he has many obstacles thrown in his path by the prejudice against him as a colored man; but he long since resolved that he would reach the highest round in the ladder. His career may well be imitated.

"Would you wrest the wreath of fame
From the hand of Fate;
Would you write a deathless name
With the good and great;
Would you bless your fellow-men,
Heart and soul imbue
With the holy task,--why, then
Paddle your own canoe."

Mr. Simpson is of small figure, unmixed in blood, has a rather mild and womanly countenance, firm and resolute eye, is gentlemanly in appearance, and intelligent in conversation.

## JEAN PIERRE BOYER.

JEAN PIERRE BOYER was born at Port au Prince on the 2d of February, 1776; received in Paris the advantages of European culture; fought under Rigaud against Toussaint; and in consequence of the success of the latter, quitted the island. Boyer returned to Hayti in Leclerc's expedition: he, however, separated from the French general-in-chief, placed himself at the head of his own color, and aided in vindicating the claims of his race to freedom in the last struggle with the French. On the death of Dessalines, Christophe, already master of the north, sought to take the south out of the hands of Petion. Boyer assisted his fellow-mulatto in driving off the black general. This act endeared him to the former. Gratitude, as well as regard to the common interest, gave Boyer the president's chair, on the death of Petion. Raised to that dignity, he employed his power and his energies to complete those economical and administrative reforms with which he had already been connected under his predecessor. To labor for the public good was the end of his life. In this worthy enterprise he was greatly assisted, no less by his knowledge than his moderation. Well acquainted with the character of the people that he was called to govern, conversant with all the interests of the state, he had it in his power to effect his purpose by mild as well as judicious measures. Yet were the wounds deep which he had to heal; and he could accomplish in a brief period only a small part of that which it will require generations to carry to perfection. At the death of Christophe, in 1820, Boyer was proclaimed president of the north and south. In 1822, the Spanish part of the island, with its own accord, joined the republic; and thus, from Cape Tiburn to Cape Engano, Hayti was peacefully settled under one government, with Boyer at its head. At length, in 1825, after the recognition of Hayti by others, the French, under Charles X., sold to its inhabitants the rights which they had won by their swords, for the sum of one hundred and fifty millions of francs, to be paid as an indemnity to the old planters. The peace with France created a more fraternal feeling between the two countries, and Hayti now began to regain her ancient commercial advantages, and every thing seemed prosperous. In the year 1843, a party opposed to the president made its appearance, which formed itself into a conspiracy to overthrow the government. Seeing that he could not make head against it, Boyer, in disgust, took leave of the people in a dignified manner, and retired to Jamaica, where, a few years since, he died.

Though called a mulatto, Boyer was nearly black, and his long residence in Europe gave him a polish in manners foreign to the island. He was a brave man, a good soldier, and proved himself a statesman of no ordinary ability. When he came into power, the mountains were filled with Maroons, headed by a celebrated chief named Gomar. Regaud and Petion had tried in vain to rid the country of these brigands. Boyer soon broke up their strongholds, dispersed them, and finally destroyed or brought them all under subjection. By his good judgment, management, and humanity, he succeeded in uniting the whole island under one government, and gained the possession of what Christophe had exhausted himself with efforts to obtain, and what Petion had sighed for, without daring to cherish a single hope that its attainment could be accomplished. Boyer was blameless in his private life.

# JAMES M'CUNE SMITH, M. D.

UNABLE to get justice done him in the educational institutions of his native country, James M'Cune Smith turned his face towards a foreign land. He graduated with distinguished honors at the University of Glasgow, Scotland, where he received his diploma of M. D. For the last twenty-five years he has been a practitioner in the city of New York, where he stands at the head of his profession. On his return from Europe, the doctor was warmly welcomed by his fellow-citizens, who were anxious to pay due deference to his talents; since which time, he has justly been esteemed among the leading men of his race on the American continent. When the natural ability of the negro was assailed, some years ago, in New York, Dr. Smith came forward as the representative of the black man, and his essays on the comparative anatomy and physiology of the races, read in the discussion, completely vindicated the character of the negro, and placed the author among the most logical and scientific writers in the country.

The doctor has contributed many valuable papers to the different journals published by colored men during the last quarter of a century. The New York dailies have also received aid from him during the same period. History, antiquity, bibliography, translation, criticism, political economy, statistics,--almost every department of knowledge,--receive emblazon from his able, ready, versatile, and unwearied pen. The emancipation of the slave, and the elevation of the free colored people, has claimed the greatest share of his time as a writer. The following, from the doctor, will give but a poor idea of his style:--
"FREEDOM--LIBERTY.

"Freedom and liberty are not synonyms. Freedom is an essence; liberty, an accident. Freedom is born within man; liberty may be conferred on him. Freedom is progressive; liberty is circumscribed. Freedom is the gift of God; liberty, the creature of society. Liberty may be taken away from man; but on whatsoever soul freedom may alight, the course of that soul is thenceforth onward and upward; society, customs, laws, armies, are but as withes in its giant grasp, if they oppose--instruments to work its will, if they assent. Human kind welcome the birth of a free soul with reverence and shoutings, rejoicing in the advent of a fresh offshoot of the divine whole, of which this is but a part."

His article in the Anglo-African Magazine, on "Citizenship," is one of the most logical arguments ever written in this country upon that subject. In the same journal, Dr. Smith has an essay on "The Fourteenth Query of Thomas Jefferson's Notes on Virginia," not surpassed by any thing which we have seen. These are the result of choice study, of nice observation, of fine feeling, of exquisite fancy, of consummate art, and the graceful tact of the scholar. Space will not allow us to select the many choice bits that we could cull from the writings of James M'Cune Smith.

The law of labor is equally binding on genius and mediocrity. The mind and body rarely visit this earth of ours so exactly fitted to each other, and so perfectly harmonizing together, as to rise without effort, and command in the affairs of men. It is not in the power of every one to become great. No great approximation, even toward that which is easiest attained, can ever be accomplished without the exercise of much thought and vigor of action; and thus is demonstrated the supremacy of that law which gives excellence only when earned, and assigns to labor its unfailing reward.

It is this energy of character, industry, and labor, combined with great intellectual powers, which has given Dr. Smith so much influence in New York. As a speaker, he is eloquent, and, at times, brilliant, but always clear and to the point. In stature, the doctor is not tall, but thick, and somewhat inclined to corpulency. He has a fine and well-developed head, broad and lofty brow, round, full face, firm mouth, and an eye that dazzles. In blood, he appears to be rather more Anglo-Saxon than African.

## BISHOP PAYNE.

TEACHER of a small school at Charleston, South Carolina, in the year 1834, Daniel A. Payne felt the oppressive hand of slavery too severely upon him, and he quitted the southern Sodom and came north. After going through a regular course of theological studies at Gettysburg Seminary, he took up his residence at Baltimore, where he soon distinguished himself as a preacher in the African Methodist denomination. He was several years since elected bishop, and is now located in the State of Ohio.

Bishop Payne is a scholar and a poet; having published, in 1850, a volume of his productions, which created considerable interest for the work, and gave the author a standing among literary men. His writings are characterized by sound reasoning and logical conclusions, and show that he is well read. The bishop is devotedly attached to his downtrodden race, and is constantly urging upon them self-elevation. After President Lincoln's interview with the committee of colored men at Washington, and the colonization scheme recommended to them, and the appearance of Mr. Pomeroy's address to the free blacks, Bishop Payne issued the following note of advice, which was published in the Weekly Anglo-African:--

"To the Colored People of the United States.

"MEN, BRETHREN, SISTERS: A crisis is upon us which no one can enable us to meet, conquer, and convert into blessings for all concerned, but that God who builds up one nation and breaks down another.

"For more than one generation, associations of white men, entitled Colonization Societies, have been engaged in plans and efforts for our expatriation; these have been met sometimes by denunciations, sometimes by ridicule, often by argument; but now the American government has assumed the work and responsibility of colonizing us in some foreign land within the torrid zone, and is now maturing measures to consummate this scheme of expatriation.

"But let us never forget that there is a vast difference between voluntary associations of men and the legally constituted authorities of a country; while the former may be held in utter contempt, the latter must always be respected. To do so is a moral and religious, as well as a political duty.

"The opinions of the government are based upon the ideas, that white men and colored men cannot live together as equals in the same country; and that unless a voluntary and peaceable separation is effected now, the time must come when there will be a war of extermination between the two races.

"Now, in view of these opinions and purposes of the government, what shall we do? My humble advice is, before all, and first of all,--even before we say yea or nay,--let us seek from the mouth of God. Let every heart be humbled, and every knee bent in prayer before him. Throughout all this land of our captivity, in all this house of our bondage, let our cries ascend perpetually to Heaven for aid and direction.

"To your knees, I say, O ye oppressed and enslaved ones of this Christian republic, to your knees, and be there.

"Before the throne of God, if nowhere else, the black man can meet his white brother as an equal, and be heard.

"It has been said that he is the God of the white man, and not of the black. This is horrible blasphemy --a lie from the pit that is bottomless--believe it not--no--never. Murmur not against the Lord on account of the cruelty and injustice of man. His almighty arm is already stretched out against slavery --against every man, every constitution, and every union that upholds it. His avenging chariot is now moving over the bloody fields of the doomed south, crushing beneath its massive wheels the very foundations of the blasphemous system. Soon slavery shall sink like Pharaoh--even like that brazen-hearted tyrant, it shall sink to rise no more forever.

"Haste ye, then, O, hasten to your God; pour the sorrows of your crushed and bleeding hearts into his sympathizing bosom. It is true that 'on the side of the oppressor there is power'--the power of the purse and the power of the sword. That is terrible. But listen to what is still more terrible: on the side of the oppressed there is the strong arm of the Lord, the Almighty God of Abraham, and Isaac, and Jacob-- before his redeeming power the two contending armies, hostile to each other, and hostile to you, are like chaff before the whirlwind.

"Fear not, but believe. He who is for you is more than they who are against you. Trust in him--hang upon his arm--go, hide beneath the shadow of his wings.

"O God! Jehovah-jireh! wilt thou not hear us? We are poor, helpless, unarmed, despised. Is it not time for thee to hear the cry of the needy--to judge the poor of the people--to break in pieces the oppressor.

"Be, O, be unto us what thou wast unto Israel in the land of Egypt, our Counsellor and Guide--our Shield and Buckler--our Great Deliverer--our Pillar of cloud by day--our Pillar of fire by night!

"Stand between us and our enemies, O thou angel of the Lord! Be unto us a shining light--to our enemies, confusion and impenetrable darkness. Stand between us till this Red Sea be crossed, and thy redeemed, now sighing, bleeding, weeping, shall shout and sing, for joy, the bold anthem of the free."

A deep vein of genuine piety pervades nearly all the productions of Bishop Payne. As a pulpit orator, he stands deservedly high. In stature, he is rather under the medium size, about three fourths African, rather sharper features than the average of his race, and appears to be about fifty years of age. He is very popular, both as a writer and a speaker, with his own color. The moral, social, and political standard of the black man has been much elevated by the influence of Bishop Payne.

# WILLIAM STILL.

THE long connection of Mr. Still with the anti-slavery office, in a city through which fugitive slaves had to pass in their flight from bondage, and the deep interest felt by him for the freedom and general welfare of his race, have brought him prominently before the public. It would not be good policy to say how many persons passed through his hands while on their way to the north or the British dominions, even if we knew. But it is safe to say that no man has been truer to the fleeing slave than he. In the first town where I stopped in Canada, while on a visit there a year since, I took a walk through the market one Saturday morning, and saw a large sprinkling of men and women who had escaped from the south. As soon as it was understood that I was from "the States," I was surrounded and overwhelmed with inquiries about places and persons. A short, stout, full-faced, energetically talking woman, looking me fairly in the eyes, said, "Were you ever in Philadelphia, sonny?" I answered that I had been there. "Did you know Mr. Still?" "Yes," said I: "do you know him?" "God love your heart! I reckon I does. He put me fru dat city on a swingin' limb, dat he did. Ah! he's a man dat can be depended on." This was only the opening; for as soon as it was known that I was well acquainted with William Still, the conversation turned entirely upon him, and I was surprised to see so many before me whom he had assisted. And though there were some present who complained of other Underground Railroad conductors, not a single word was uttered against

Mr. Still; but all united in the strongest praise of him. In every town that I visited during a stay of ten weeks in Canada, I met persons who made feeling inquiries after him, and I was glad to find that all regarded him as a benefactor. Mr. Still is well educated, has good talents, and has cultivated them. He is an interesting and forcible writer, and some of the stories of escaped slaves, which he has contributed to the press, will challenge criticism. A correspondent of one of the public journals sent the following account to his paper of all interview which he had with Mr. Still the day previous:--

"We sat down to talk. The ultimate destiny of the black man was discussed, our host opening that his struggle for a habitation and a name must be in America. He said that his people were attached to the republic, notwithstanding many disadvantages imposed upon them, their hope being strong that patience and good citizenship would eventually soften the prejudices of the whites. Tempered as they were to our habits and climate, it would be cruel to place them on a strand but dimly known, where, surrounded by savages, they might become savage themselves.

"There was to us a sincere pleasure in our host's discourse. He is one of the leading public men among his people, and has much of the ease and polish peculiar to the well-bred Caucasian. He laughed at times, but never boisterously, and in profounder moments threw a telling solemnity into his tone and expression. When the head was averted, we heard, in well-modulated speech, such vigorous sentences and thoughtful remarks, that the identity of the speaker with the proscribed race was half forgotten; but the biased eyesight revealed only a dusky son of Ham. On a 'what-not' table were clustered a number of books. Most of them were anti-slavery publications, although there were several volumes of sermons, and a few philosophical and historical books. We turned the conversation to literature. He was well acquainted with the authors he had read, and ventured some criticisms, indicative of study. From the earnestness of the man, it seemed that the interests of his race were very dear to him.

"It is but just to say, that he has passed many years in constant companionship with Caucasians."

Mr. Still is somewhat tall, neat in figure and person, has a smiling face, is unadulterated in blood, and gentlemanly in his intercourse with society. He is now extensively engaged in the stove and fuel trade, keeps five or six men employed, and has the patronage of some of the first families of Philadelphia. He has the entire confidence of all who know and appreciate his moral worth and business talents.

## EDWIN M. BANNISTER.

EDWIN M. BANNISTER was born in the town of St. Andrew, New Brunswick, and lost his father when only six years old. He attended the grammar school in his native place, and received a better education than persons generally in his position. From early childhood he seems to have had a fancy for painting, which showed itself in the school room and at home. He often drew portraits of his school-fellows, and the master not unfrequently found himself upon the slate, where Edwin's success was so manifest that the likeness would call forth merriment from the boys, and create laughter at the expense of the teacher. At the death of his mother, when still in his minority, he was put out to live with the Hon. Harris Hatch, a wealthy lawyer, the proprietor of a fine farm some little distance in the country. In his new home Edwin did not lose sight of his drawing propensities, and though the family had nothing in the way of models except two faded portraits, kept more as relics than for their intrinsic value, he nevertheless practised upon them, and often made the copy look more life-like than the original. On the barn doors, fences, and every place where drawings could be made, the two ancient faces were to be seen pictured. When the family were away on the Sabbath at church, the young artist would take possession of the old Bible, and copy its crude engravings, then replace it upon the dusty shelf, feeling an inward gratification, that, instead of satisfying the inclination, only gave him fresh zeal to hunt for now models. By the great variety of drawings which he had made on paper, and the correct sketches taken, young Bannister gained considerable reputation in the lawyer's family, as well as in the neighborhood. Often, after the household had retired at night, the dim glimmer from the lean tallow candle was seen through the attic chamber window. It was there that the genius of the embryo artist was struggling for development. Nearly every wall in the dwelling had designs or faces pencilled upon it, and many were the complaints that the women made against the lad. At last he turned his steps towards Boston, with the hope that he might get a situation with a painter, never dreaming that his color would be a barrier to the accomplishment of such an object. Weeks were spent by the friendless, homeless, and penniless young man, and every artist had seen his face and heard his wish to become a painter. But visiting these establishments brought nothing to sustain nature, and Mr. Bannister took up the business of a hair-dresser, merely as a means of getting bread, but determined to leave it as soon as an opening presented itself with an artist. The canvas, the paint, the easel, and the pallet were brought in, and the hair-dressing saloon was turned into a studio.

There is a great diversity of opinion with regard to genius, many mistaking talent for genius. Talent is strength and subtilty of mind; genius is mental inspiration and delicacy of feeling. Talent possesses vigor and acuteness of penetration, but is surpassed by the vivid intellectual conceptions of genius. The former is skilful and bold, the latter aspiring and gentle. But talent excels in practical sagacity; and hence those striking contrasts so often witnessed in the world--the triumph of talent through its adroit and active energies, and the adversities of genius in the midst of its boundless but unattainable aspirations.

Mr. Bannister possesses genius, which is now showing itself in his studio in Boston; for he has long since thrown aside the scissors and the comb, and transfers the face to the canvas, instead of taking the hair from the head. His portraits are correct representations of the originals, and he is daily gaining admirers of his talent and taste. He has painted several pictures from his own designs, which exhibit his genius. "Wall Street at Home," represents the old gent, seated in his easy chair, boots off and slippers on, and intently reading the last news. The carpet with its variegated colors, the hat upon the table, the cloak thrown carelessly across a chair, and the pictures hanging on the walls, are all brought out with their lights and shades. A beautiful landscape, representing summer, with the blue mountains in the distance, the heated sky, and the foliage to match, is another of his pieces. It is indeed commendable in Mr. Bannister, that he has thus far overcome the many obstacles thrown in his way by his color, and made himself an honor to his race.

Mr. Bannister is spare-made, slim, with an interesting cast of countenance, quick in his walk, and easy in his manners. He is a lover of poetry and the classics, and is always hunting up some new model for his gifted pencil and brush. He has a picture representing "Cleopatra waiting to receive Marc Antony," which I regret that I did not see. I am informed, however, that it is a beautifully-executed picture. Mr. Bannister has a good education, is often called upon to act as secretary to public meetings, and is not by any means a bad speaker, when on the platform. Still young, enterprising, and spirited, we shall be mistaken if Edwin M. Bannister does not yet create a sensation in our country as an artist.

## LEONARD A. GRIMES.

LEONARD A. GRIMES is a native of Leesburg, Loudon county, Va., and was born in 1815. He went to Washington when a boy, and was first employed in a butcher's shop, and afterwards in an apothecary's establishment. He subsequently hired himself out to a slaveholder, whose confidence he soon gained. Accompanying his employer in some of his travels in the remote Southern States, young Grimes had an opportunity of seeing the different phases of slave life; and its cruelty created in his mind an early hatred to the institution which has never abated. He could not resist the appeals of the bondmen for aid in making their escape to a land of freedom, and consequently was among the first to take stock in the Underground Railroad. After saving money enough by his earnings, he purchased a hack and horses, and became a hackman in the city of Washington. In his new vocation, Mr. Grimes met with success, and increased his business until he was the owner of a number of carriages and horses, and was considered one of the foremost men in his line. During all this time he never lost sight of the slave, and there is no telling how many he put on the road to Canada. A poor woman and her seven children were about being carried away to the far south by the slave-trader. Her husband, a free black, sought out Leonard A. Grimes, and appealed to his humanity, and not in vain; for in less than forty-eight hours, the hackman penetrated thirty miles into Virginia, and, under cover of night, brought out the family. The husband, wife, and little ones, a few days after, breathed the free air of Canada. Mr. Grimes was soon suspected, arrested, tried, and sentenced to two years in the state prison, at Richmond. Here he remained; and the close, dank air, the gloom, the high, dull, cold, stone walls, the heavy fetters upon his limbs, the entire lack of any thing external to distract his thoughts from his situation, all together, produced a feeling of depression he had never known before. It was at this time that Mr. Grimes "felt," as he says, 'that great spiritual change which makes all things new for the soul." From that hour he became a preacher to his keepers, and, as far as he was allowed, to his fellow-prisoners. This change lightened his confinement, and caused him to feel that he was sent there to do his Master's will.

At the expiration of his imprisonment, Mr. Grimes returned to Washington, and employed himself in driving a furniture car, and jobbing about the city. Feeling himself called to preach, he underwent the required examination, received a license, and, without quitting his employment, preached as occasion offered. Not long after this, he removed to New Bedford, Mass.,where he resided two years. There was in Boston a small congregation, worshipping in a little room, but without a regular preacher. An invitation was extended to Mr. Grimes to become their pastor. He accepted, came to Boston, and, under his ministration, the society increased so rapidly that a larger house was soon needed. A lot was purchased, the edifice begun, and now they have a beautiful church, capable of seating six or seven hundred persons. The cost of the building, including the land, was $13,000; all of which, except $2,000, has been paid. We need not say that this was accomplished through the untiring exertions of Mr. Grimes. Besides his labors in the society, he was often engaged in aiding fugitive slaves in the redemption of their relations from the servitude of the south. During his fourteen years' residence in Boston, he has had $6,000 pass through his hands, for the benefit of that class of persons. In action he is always--

"Upward, onward, pressing forward
Till each bondman's chains shall fall,
Till the flag that floats above us
Liberty proclaims to all."

In 1854, Mr. Grimes became conspicuously connected with the fugitive slave Anthony Burns. Mainly through his efforts the latter gained his freedom. The pastor of the Twelfth Baptist Church is, emphatically, a practical man. Nearly all public meetings are held either in his church or vestry, he taking a suitable part in every thing that tends to the welfare of his race. "Brother" Grimes is above the middle size, good looking, has a full face, a countenance which has the appearance of one who has seen no trouble, and rather more Anglo-Saxon than African.

He is polite in his manners, and genteel in his personal appearance. As a preacher, he is considered sound, and well versed in theology. He is regarded as one of the ablest men in prayer in Boston. His sermons are characterized by deep feeling and good sense. No man in the city has fewer enemies or more friends than Leonard A. Grimes.

## PRESIDENT GEFFRARD.

FABRE GEFFRARD, born at Cayes, in the year 1806, was the son of a general who had shown himself humane under Dessalines, and had been with Petion, one of the chief promoters of the constitution of 1806. Left early an orphan, young Geffrard entered the army at the age of fifteen, and only after twenty-two years' service obtained his captain's commission. He took part --unwisely, as events proved--in the revolution of 1843, which overturned the able but indolent Boyer, and distinguished himself at the head of a small body of troops against the government forces, deceiving them as to his numbers by the rapidity of his movements, and as to his resources by supplying provisions to his famished enemies at a time when he himself was short of rations. When the revolution, which had originated with the most impatient of the mulattoes, led in turn to a rising of that portion of the blacks who represented absolute barbarism, and whose axiom was that every mulatto should be exterminated, Geffrard marched against and defeated the black leader, Arcaau; but, true to that humanity which seems the very basis of his character, we find him in turn defending the middle classes from the blacks, and the insurgent blacks, when taken prisoners, from the National Guard. He became lieutenant-general during these movements; but General Riche, who was made president in 1846, and who bore Geffrard a grudge for having on a former occasion made him a prisoner, sent him before a court martial, which, in Hayti, means sending one to death. Through the adroitness, however, of Riche's minister of war, the general was acquitted. The president of the court martial was Soulouque, who seems to have imbibed, on this occasion, a strange friendship for the man whose life he had been the means of preserving, and who thus spared him, in an otherwise unaccountable manner, during his subsequent rule, and even forced on him the title of duke, which Geffrard did not care to assume. In two disastrous wars which he undertook, in 1849 and in 1855-6, against the Dominican republic, Geffrard alone won credit. In the former he was wounded at the head of the division; in both, by his courage, his activity, his cheerfulness, and above all, by his anxious care for the welfare of his soldiers, he exhibited the most striking contrast to Soulouque's imbecile generalship and brutal indifference to the safety of others.

In 1858, Soulouque, seeing that Geffrard's popularity was becoming great, sought an opportunity to have him arrested. Spies were placed near him. The general, however, was warned of his danger, and he knew that nothing was to be hoped for from Soulouque's ferocity when once aroused by jealousy. Just then, the emissaries of a conspiracy, formed in the valley of the Artibonite, beyond the mountain chain which forms the backbone of the island, were in Port au Prince in search of a leader. They addressed themselves to Geffrard. The cup of Soulouque's tyranny was full. Geffrard listened to their solicitations, but was barely able, by the aid of a friend, to escape in an open boat, on the very night when be was to have been arrested. He succeeded in reaching St. Mark, but found that the people were not ready for a revolution. He repaired to Gonaives, where the inhabitants were thoroughly ripe for a change of rulers. Thus six men coming by sea, met by three on land, were sufficient to carry the place without the shedding of a drop of blood. On the 22d of December, he issued two proclamations, the one abolishing the empire, the other establishing a republic. From thence he proceeded to St. Mark, where he was enthusiastically welcomed by all classes, the army joining him to a man. With two thousand men he started for Port au Prince, the capital. Soulouque, in the mean time, gathered his forces, amounting to six thousand well-drilled troops, and set out to meet his rival, but soon found that his army could not be relied on, and he returned amid the hootings of the people. The emperor was permitted to take refuge in the French consulate, and from thence took passage in an English steamer for Jamaica. Geffrard entered Port au Prince in triumph; the constitution of 1846 was adopted, and an election held which chose Geffrard president for life, with the privilege of nominating his successor. All agree that he is a good man. His great aim appears to be the moral, social, and intellectual improvement of the people.

Most of the army have been disbanded; and those retained are better fed, better paid, and clothed in a more suitable manner. New firearms have been introduced, reforms instituted both in the government and the army, agriculture and commerce encouraged, old roads repaired and new ones built. His state papers show him to be a man of superior natural abilities, and we believe that he is destined to do more for Hayti and her people than any ruler since the days of

Toussaint L'Ouverture. Geffrard is a grief in color (nearly black), of middle height, slim in figure, a pleasing countenance, sparkling eye, gray hair, fifty-six years of age, limbs supple by bodily exercise, a splendid horseman, and liberal to the arts, even to extravagance. Possessing a polished education, he is gentlemanly in his conversation and manners. His democratic ideas induce him to dress without ornaments of any kind. Soon after assuming the presidency, he resolved to encourage immigration, and issued an address to the colored Americans, filled with patriotic and sympathetic feeling for his race.

# GEORGE B. VASHON.

PASSING through the schools of Pittsburg, his native place, and graduating at Oberlin College with the degree of Master of Arts, George B. Vashon started in life with the advantage of a good education. He studied law with Hon. Walter Forward, and was admitted to the bar in 1847. He soon after visited Hayti, where he remained nearly three years, returning home in 1850. Called to a professorship in New York Central College, Mr. Vashon discharged the duties of the office with signal ability. A gentleman--a graduate of that institution, now a captain in the federal army --told the writer that he and several of his companions, who had to recite to Professor Vashon, made it a practice for some length of time to search Greek, Latin, and Hebrew, for phrases and historical incidents, and would then question the professor, with the hope of "running him on a snag." "But," said he, "we never caught him once, and we came to the conclusion that be was the best-read man in the college." Literature has a history, and few histories can compare with it in importance, significance and moral grandeur. There is, therefore, a great price to pay for literary attainments, which will have an inspiring and liberalizing influence--a price not in silver and gold, but in thorough mental training. This training will give breadth of view, develop strength of character and a comprehensive spirit, by which the ever-living expressions of truth and principle in the past may be connected with those of a like character in the present.

Mr. Vashon seems to have taken this view of what constitutes the thorough scholar, and has put his theory into practice. All of the productions of his pen show the student and man of literature. But he is not indebted alone to culture, for be possesses genius of no mean order-- poetic genius, far superior to many who have written and published volumes. As Dryden said of Shakspeare, "he needed not the spectacles of books to read Nature; he looked inward, and found her there." The same excellence appertains to his poetical description of the beautiful scenery and climate of Hayti, in his "Vincent Oge." His allusion to Columbus's first visit to the island is full of solemn grandeur:--

> "The waves dash brightly on thy shore,
> Fair island of the southern seas,
> As bright in joy as when, of yore,
> They gladly hailed the Genoese--
> That daring soul who gave to Spain
> A world-last trophy of her reign."

Our limited space will not permit our giving more of this, or other poems of Mr. Vashon. The following extract from his admirable essay in the Anglo-African Magazine, entitled, "The Successive Advances of Astronomy," is characteristic of his prose:--

"The next important step recorded in the annals of astronomy was the effort to reform the calendar by means of the bissextile year. This effort was made at the time when Julius Caesar was chief pontiff at Rome. It is noteworthy, as being the only valuable contribution made to astronomical science by the Romans; and, even in this matter, Caesar acted under the guidance of the Grecian astronomer Sosigenes. We are not to. suppose, however, that the Romans were totally indifferent to the subject of astronomy. We are informed by Cicero, in his elegant treatise concerning 'Old Age,' that Caius Gallus was accustomed to spend whole days and nights in making observations upon the heavenly bodies, and that he took pleasure in predicting to his friends the eclipses of the sun and moon a long time before they occurred. Besides, in the 'Scipio's Dream' of the same author, we find, in the course of an admirable dissertation upon the immortality of the soul, an account of a terrestrial system, according to which our earth was the central body, around which the concave sphere of the starry heavens revolved; while, in the space between the Moon, Venus, Mercury, the Sun, Mars, Jupiter, and Saturn moved with retrograde courses, in the order here mentioned. In fact, this system was the one which was afterwards adopted, elaborated, and zealously maintained by the famous Ptolemy of Alexandria, and which has ever since borne his name. To Ptolemy, then, who flourished about the commencement of the second century, the world is indebted for the first complete system of astronomy that secured the approbation of all the learned. This it was enabled to do by the ingenious, although not perfect, explanation which it gave of the planetary movements, by supposing these bodies to move in circles whose centres had an easterly motion along an imaginary circles. Thus these epicycles, as the circles were called, moving along the imaginary circle, or deferent, cause the planets to have, at times, an apparent easterly direction, at other times a westerly one, and at other times, again, to appear stationary. Thus recommended, the Ptolemaic system continued to gain adherents, until the irruptions of the Huns under Alaric and Attila, and the destruction of the celebrated library at Alexandria by the fanatical and turbulent Christians of that city, laid waste the fair domains of science. Being thus driven from the places where Learning had fixed her favorite seats, it took refuge with the Arabs, who preserved it with watchful care, until happier times restored it to Europe. It returned with the conquering Moors who established themselves in Spain, was brought again under the notice of the Christian states in the thirteenth century, through the patronage of the emperor Frederic II. of Germany, and Alphonso X. of Castile, and flourished more than two hundred years longer, without any rival to dispute its claims to correctness."

Mr. Vashon is of mixed blood, in stature of medium size, rather round face, with a somewhat solemn countenance,--a man of few words,--needs, to be drawn out, to be appreciated. While visiting a distinguished colored gentleman at Rochester, N. Y., some years ago, the host, who happened to be a wit as well as an orator, invited in "Professor T."--a man ignorant of education, but filled with big talk and high-sounding words without understanding their meaning--to entertain Mr. Vashon, intending it as a joke. "Professor T." used all the language that he was master of, but to no purpose: the man of letters sat still, listened, gazed at the former, but did not dispute any point raised. The uneducated professor, feeling that he had been imposed upon, called Mr. D. one side, and in a whisper said, "Are you sure that this is an educated Man.? I fear that he is an impostor; for I tried, but could not call him out."

## ROBERT MORRIS.

ABOUT the year 1837, Ellis Gray Loring, Esq., took into his office, as an errand boy, a colored lad of fifteen years of age. The youngster had a better education than those generally of his age, which showed that he had been attentive at school. He was not long in his new situation ere he began to exhibit a liking for the contents of the sheepskin-covered books that stood around on the shelves, and lay upon the baize-covered tables. Mr. Loring, seeing the aptitude of the lad, inquired if he wanted to become a lawyer, and was answered in the affirmative. From that moment the errand boy became the student, and studied with an earnestness not often equalled. At scarcely twenty-one years of age he was admitted to the Boston bar. This was Robert Morris. With all the prejudice before him, he kept steadily on, resolving that he would overcome the negro-hate which stood in the way of his efforts to prosecute his profession. Gradually he grew in practice, until most of his fellow-members forgot his color in the admiration of his eloquence and business talent. Mr. Morris is of unmixed blood, but not black. Small in stature, a neat figure, smiling face, always dressed with the greatest care, gentlemanly in manner and conversation, his influence has been felt in behalf of his race. He is an interesting speaker, quick in his gestures, ardent in his feelings, and enthusiastic in what he undertakes. He rather inclines to a military life, and has, on more than one occasion, attempted the organization of an independent company.

At the presentation of the portrait of John T. Hilton to the Prince Hall Grand Lodge of Boston, Mr. Morris made a speech, of which the following is an extract:--

"I wish we could point to well-executed likenesses of those old colored heroes of revolutionary memory, who so nobly, patriotically, and willingly, side by side with their white brethren, fought, bled, and died to secure freedom and independence to America.

"It would be a source of continual pleasure could we have in some public room pictures true to life of those intrepid heroes, Denmark Veazie and Nat Turner, whose very names were a terror to oppressors; who, conceiving the sublime idea of freedom for themselves and their race, animated by a love of liberty of which they had been ruthlessly deprived, made an attempt to sever their bonds; and though, in such attempts to open the prison doors of slavery and let the oppressed go free, they were unsuccessful, their efforts and determination were none the less noble and heroic. In the future history of our country, their names to us will shine as brightly as that of the glorious old hero, who, with his colored and white followers, so strategically captured Harper's Ferry, and touched a chord in the life of our country that will vibrate throughout the land, and will not cease until the last fetter has been struck from the limbs of the last bondman in the nation; and though the bodies of these heroes he mouldering in the clay, their souls are 'marching on.'

"I never visit our 'Cradle of Liberty,' and look at the portraits that grace its walls, without thinking that the selection is sadly incomplete, because the picture of the massacred Crispus Attucks is not there. He was the first martyr in the Boston massacre of March 5, 1770, when the British soldiers were drawn up in line on King (now State) Street, to intimidate the Boston populace. On that eventful day, a band of patriots, led by Attucks, marched from Dock Square to drive the redcoats from the vicinity of the old State House. Emboldened by the courageous conduct of this colored hero, the band pressed forward, and in attempting to wrest a musket from one of the British soldiers, Attucks was shot. His was the first blood that crimsoned the pavement of King Street, and by the sacrifice of his life, he awoke that fiery hatred of British oppression which culminated in the declaration of American independence. At this late day a portrait of this hero cannot be had; but our children will live to see the day when the people of this commonwealth mindful of their deep and lasting obligation will, through their legislature, appropriate a sufficient sum wherewith to erect a suitable monument to preserve the memory of Attucks, and mark the spot where he fell."

Mr. Morris deserves great credit for having fought his way up to his present position. Rumor says that his profession has paid him well, and that he is now a man of property. If so, we are glad; for the poet writes, "If thou wouldst have influence, put money in thy purse."

## WILLIAM J. WILSON.

IN the columns of Frederick Douglass's paper, the Anglo-African Magazine, and the Weekly Anglo-African, has appeared at times, over the signature of "Ethiop," some of the raciest and most amusing essays to be found in the public journals of this country. As a sketch writer of historical scenes and historical characters,--choosing his own subjects, suggested by his own taste or sympathies,--few men are capable of greater or more successful efforts than William J. Wilson. In his imaginary visit to the "Afric-American Picture Gallery," he gives the following sketch of the head of Phillis Wheatley.

"This picture hangs in the north-east corner of the gallery, and in good light, and is so decidedly one of the finest in the collection, whether viewed in an artistic light or in point of fact, that it is both a constant charm and study for me. The features, though indicative of a delicate organization, are of the most pleasing cast. The facial angle contains full ninety degrees; the forehead is finely formed, and the brain large; the nose is long, and the nostrils thin, while the eyes, though not large, are well set. To this may be added a small mouth, with lips prettily turned, and a chin--that perfection of beauty in the female face --delicately tapered from a throat and neck that are of themselves perfection. The whole make-up of this face is an index of healthy intellectual powers, combined with an active temperament, over which has fallen a slight tinge of religious pensiveness. Thus hangs Phillis Wheatley before you in the Afric-American Picture Gallery; and if we scrutinize her more closely through her career and her works, we shall find her truly an extraordinary person. Stolen at the tender age of seven years from the fond embraces of a mother, whose image never once faded from her memory, and ferried over in the vile slave ship from Afric's sunny clime to the cold shores of America, and sold under the hammer to a Boston merchant--a delicate child, a girl, alone, desolate; a chilly, dreary world before her, a chain on her feet, and a thorn in her bosom, and an iron mask on her head, what chance, what opportunity was there for her to make physical,moral, or mental progress? In these respects, how get up to, or keep pace with, other and more favored people?--how get in the advance?--how ascend, at last, without a single competitor, the highest scale of human eminence? Phillis Wheatley did all, and more than this. A sold thing, a bought chattel at seven years, she mastered, notwithstanding, the English language in sixteen months. She carried on with her friends and acquaintances an extensive and elegant epistolary correspondence at twelve years of age, composed her first poem at fourteen, became a proficient Latin scholar at seventeen, and published in England her book of poems, dedicated to the Countess of Huntington, at nineteen; and with the mantle of just fame upon her shoulders, sailed from America to England to receive the meed due to her learning, her talents, and her virtues, at twenty-two. What one of America's paler daughters, contemporary with her, with all the advantages that home, fortune, friends, and favor bring,--what one ascended so far up the hill of just fame at any age? I have searched in vain to find the name upon the literary page of our country's record.

> "O Wheatley!
> What degrading hand, what slavish chain,
> What earthly power could link thy nobler soul
> To baser things, and check its eagle flight?
> Angel of purity, child of beauteous song,
> Thy harp still hangs within our sight,
> To cheer, though thou art gone."

The succeeding extract from his poem "The Coming Man" is very suggestive, especially at this time.

> "I break the chains that have been clanging
> Down through the dim vault of ages;
> I gird up my strength--mind and arm,--
> And prepare for the terrible conflict.
> I am to war with principalities, powers, wrongs
> With oppressions,--with all that curse humanity.
> I am resolved. 'Tis more than half my task;
> 'Twas the great need of all my past existence.
> The glooms that have so long shrouded me,
> Recede as vapor from the new presence,
> And the light-gleam--it must be, life--
> So brightens and spreads its pure rays before,
> That I read my mission as 'twere a book.
> It is life; life in which none but men--
> Not those who only wear the form--can live
> To give this life to the World; to make men
> Out of the thews and sinews of oppressed slaves."

Mr. Wilson is a teacher, and whether the following is drawn from his own experience, or not, we are left to conjecture.

# THE TEACHER AND HIS PUPIL.

SCENE.--School Room. School in session.

Dramatis Personæ.

TEACHER. A bachelor rising thirty.

PUPIL. A beautiful girl of sixteen.

I see that curling and high-archéd brow.
"Scold thee?" Ay, that I will.
Pouting I see thee still;
Thou jade! I know that thou art laughing now!

Silence! hush! nor dare one word to mutter!
If it were e'er so gentle,
(I speak in tone parental,)
Do not thy very softest whisper utter.

I know that startled trembling all a hoax,
Thou pert and saucy thing!
I'll make thy fine ears ring
I'll pretermit thy silly, taunting jokes.

"Whip thee?" Ay, that I will, and whip thee well;
Thy chattering tongue now hold!
There, there; I will no further scold.
How down those lovely cheeks the hot tears fell!

How quickly changed! Nay, nay; come hither, child.
'Tis with kindness I would rule;
Severity's the erring fool,
Who harms the tender or excites the wild.

What! trembling yet, and shy? Nay, do not fear;
Sure, sure I'll harm thee not;
My gentlest, thine's a better lot;
So raise those azure eyes with radiant cheer.
Cheer up, then; there, now thou canst go. Retain,
I pray, within thy heart,
Not the unpleasant part
That's past. The other let remain.

To possess genius, the offspring of which ennobles the sentiments, enlarges the affections, kindles the imagination, and gives to us a view of the past, the present, and the future, is one of the highest gifts that the Creator bestows upon man. With acute powers of conception, a sparkling and lively fancy, and a quaintly curious felicity of diction, Mr. Wilson wakes us from our torpidity and coldness to a sense of our capabilities. In personal appearance he is under the middle size; his profile is more striking than his front face; he has a rather pleasing countenance, and is unmixed in race; has fine conversational powers, is genteel in his manners, and is a pleasant speaker upon the platform.

# JOHN MERCER LANGSTON.

ONE of the most promising young men of the west is John M. Langston, a native of Chillicothe, Ohio, and a graduate of Oberlin College. He studied theology and law, and, preferring the latter, was admitted to the bar, and is now successfully practising his profession.

The end of all eloquence is to sway men. It is, therefore, bound by no arbitrary rules of diction or style, formed on no specific models, and governed by no edicts of self-elected judges. It is true, there are degrees of eloquence, and equal success does not imply equal excellence. That which is adapted to sway the strongest minds of an enlightened age ought to be esteemed the most perfect, and, doubtless, should be the criterion by which to test the abstract excellence of all oratory. Mr. Langston represents the highest idea of the orator, as exemplified in the power and discourses of Sheridan in the English House of Commons, and Vergniaud in the Assembly of the Giroudists. He is not fragmentary in his speeches; but, a deep, majestic stream, he moves steadily onward, pouring forth his rich and harmonious sentences in strains of impassioned eloquence. His style is bold and energetic - full of spirit. He is profound without being hollow, and ingenious without being subtile.

Being at Oberlin a few years since, and learning that a suit was to be tried before a justice of the peace, in which Langston was counsel for the defence, I attended. Two white lawyers--one from Elyria, the other residing at Oberlin--were for the plaintiff. One day was consumed in the examination and cross-questioning of witnesses, in which the colored lawyer showed himself more than a match for his antagonists. The plaintiff's counsel moved an adjournment to the next day. The following morning the court room was full before the arrival of the presiding justice, and much interest was manifested on both sides. Langston's oratory was a model for the students at the college, and all who could leave their studies or recitations were present. When the trial commenced, it was observed that the plaintiffs had introduced a third lawyer on their side. This was an exhibition of weakness on their part, and proved the power of the "black lawyer," who stood single-handed and alone. The pleading commenced, and consumed the forenoon; the plaintiff only being heard. An adjournment for an hour occurred, and then began one of the most powerful addresses that I had heard for a long time. In vigor of thought, in imagery of style, in logical connection, in vehemence, in depth, in point, and in beauty of language, Langston surpassed his opponents, won the admiration of the jury and the audience, and, what is still better for his credit, he gained the suit. Mr. Langston's practice extends to Columbus, the capital of the state, and in the county towns, within fifty miles of his home, he is considered the most successful man at the bar.

An accomplished scholar and a good student, he displays in his speeches an amount of literary acquirements not often found in the mere business lawyer. When pleading he speaks like a man under oath, though without any starched formality of expression. The test of his success is the permanent impression which his speeches leave on the memory. They do not pass away with the excitement of the moment, but remain in the mind, with the lively colors and true proportions of the scenes which they represent. Mr. Langston is of medium size and of good figure, high and well-formed forehead, eyes full, but not prominent, mild and amiable countenance, modest deportment, strong, musical voice, and wears the air of a gentleman. He is highly respected by men of the legal profession throughout the state. He is a vigorous writer, and in the political campaigns, contributes both with speech and pen to the liberal cause. Few men in the south-west have held the black man's standard higher than John Mercer Langston.

## WILLIAM C. NELL.

No man in New England has performed more uncompensated labor for humanity, and especially for his own race, than William C. Nell. Almost from the commencement of the Liberator, and the opening of an anti-slavery office in Boston, he has been connected in some way with the cause of freedom. In 1840, Mr. Nell, in company with William Lloyd Garrison, Wendell Phillips, and Francis Jackson, signed a petition to the city government, asking it to grant equal school rights to the colored children. From that time till 1855, Mr. Nell lost no opportunity to press this question. During all this while he had to meet the frowns of the whites, who were instigated by that mean and relentless prejudice which slavery had implanted in their minds; but he went steadily on, resolving that he would not cease till equality was acknowledged in the Boston schools. In 1855 the obnoxious rule was abolished, and the colored youths admitted to the schools, without regard to complexion. On the evening of December 17 of the same year, Mr. Nell was publicly presented with a testimonial by his fellow-citizens. This consisted of a valuable gold watch. Master Frederick Lewis, on behalf of the children, addressed Mr. Nell as follows:--

"Champion of equal school rights, we hail thee. With unbounded gratitude we bow before thee. Our youthful hearts bless thee for thy incessant labors and untiring zeal in our behalf. We would fain assist in swelling thy praise, which flows from every lip; but this were a tribute far too small. Noble friend: thou hast opened for us the gate that leadeth to rich treasures; and as we pass through, Ambition lendeth us a hand--ay, she quickeneth our pace; and as, obeying her, we look through the vista of future years, we recognize bright Fame in a field of literary glory, her right hand extended with laurels of honor, to crown those who shall be most fortunate in gaining the platform whereon she standeth; while before her is spread the banquet, with viands rich and rare, that our literary hunger may be satiated. To this we aspire. To gain this we will be punctual to school, diligent in study, and well-behaved; and may we be enabled to reach the goal, that, in thy declining years, thy heart may be gladdened by what thine eye beholdeth, and it shall be like a crown of gold encircling thy head, and like a rich mantle thrown around thee, studded with jewels and precious stones.

"Kind benefactor: accept, we entreat thee, this simple token, emblem of the bright, gladsome years of youthful innocence and purity; and as thou hast befriended us, so may we ever prove faithful friends to thee. May the blessings of Heaven attend thee through life's ever-changing scenes and intricate windings, is our prayer."

Mrs. Georgiana O. Smith then presented to Mr. Nell the watch, bearing this inscription:--
"A Tribute to
WILLIAM C. NELL,
FROM THE COLORED CITIZENS OF BOSTON,
For his untiring efforts in behalf of
EQUAL SCHOOL RIGHTS,
Dec. 17, 1855."

Mrs. Smith's address was well conceived, and delivered in an eloquent and feeling manner which seemed to touch every heart and quicken every pulse. Mr. Nell responded in an able speech, recounting many of the scenes that they had passed through. William Lloyd Garrison and Wendell Phillips were both present, and addressed the meeting, showing their deep interest in the black man's rights. Besides contributing occasionally to the columns of the Liberator, Frederick Douglass's paper, the Anglo-African, and other journals, Mr. Nell is the author of the "Colored Patriots of the American Revolution," a book filled with interesting incidents connected with the history of the blacks of this country, past and present. He has also written several smaller works, all of which are humanitarian in their character. He has taken a leading part in most of the conventions and public gatherings of the colored citizens, held within the past twenty-five years. From 1835 to 1850, no public meeting was complete without William C Nell as secretary.

Deeply interested in the intellectual development and cultivation of his race, he aided in the organization of the "Adelphic Union Association," which did much good in its day. Later still, he brought into existence the "Histrionic Club," a society that encouraged reading, recitation, and social conversation. In this he drew the finest talent that Boston could produce. They gave a public representation a few years since, which was considered one of the most classic performances which has ever been witnessed. Mr. Nell is of medium height, slim, genteel figure, quick step, elastic movement, a thoughtful yet pleasant brow, thin face, and chaste in his conversation. Born in Boston, passing through her public schools, a good student, and a lover of literature, he has a cultivated understanding, and has collected together more facts, on the race with whom he is identified, than any other man of our acquaintance. An ardent admirer of Wendell Phillips, he seems as much attached to that distinguished orator as

Boswell was to Johnson. Mr. Nell's devotion to his race is not surpassed by any man living.

# JOHN SELLA MARTIN.

J. SELLA MARTIN is a native of Charlotte, North Carolina, and was born on the 27th of September, 1832. His mother was a slave, and by the laws of the state the child follows the condition of the mother. Young Martin sustained the double but incongruous relation to his owner of master and son. At the tender age of six years, the boy, together with his mother and an only sister, was taken from the old homestead at midnight, and carried to Columbus, Georgia, where they were exposed for sale. Here they were separated, the mother and daughter being purchased by one man, and Sella by another. The latter had the good fortune, however, to fall into the hands of an old bachelor, with whom he lived, in the capacity of valet de chambre, until he was eighteen years old. His opportunities, while with him, for acquiring a knowledge of books and the world generally, were far better than usually fall to the lot of the most favored house servants. Both master and slave boarded at the principal hotel in the place; and the latter, associating with other servants, and occasionally meeting travellers from the free states, obtained much valuable information respecting the north and Canada, and his owner was not a little surprised one day when a complaint came to him that his servant had been furnishing passes for slaves in the neighborhood to visit their wives. Sella was called before the master, and threatened with severe punishment if he ever wrote another pass for a Slave. About two years after this, the owner partially lost his sight, and the servant became first the reader of the morning paper, and subsequently the amanuensis in the transaction of all the master's business. An intimacy sprang up between the two, and it being for the white man's interest that his chattel should read and write correctly, the latter became in fact the pupil of the former, which accelerated his education. At the age of eighteen his owner died, and Sella was left free. But the influence of the heirs at law was sufficient to set the will aside, and the free young man, together with other slaves of the estate, was sold on the auction block, and the new owner took Sella to Mobile, where be resided till 1852, when he was again sold and taken to New Orleans. Here the subject of our sketch hired his own time, became a dealer in fruit and oysters, and succeeded in saving a little money for himself, with which he made his escape on a Mississippi steamer in December, 1855, and arrived at Chicago on the 6th of January, 1856. The great hope of his younger days had been attained, and he was now free. But Mr. Martin had seen too much of slavery to feel satisfied with merely getting his own freedom, and he therefore began the inquiry to see what he could do for those whom he had left in the prison house of bondage. While at Chicago, he made the acquaintance of Mr. H. Ford Douglass, who was just about to visit the interior of the state, to deliver a course of lectures. The latter observed by his conversation with Mr. Martin, that he possessed the elements of a good speaker, and persuaded him to join and take part in the meetings. It is said that Mr. Martin's first attempt in public was an entire failure. He often alludes to it himself, and says that the humiliation which he experienced reminded him. of the time when he was sold on the auction block--only that the former seemed the cheaper sale of the two. He was advised never to try the platform again. But his want of success on the first occasion stimulated him to new exertion, and we are told that he wrote out a speech, committed it to memory, and delivered it two days after to the satisfaction of all present. Mr. Douglass himself characterizes it as a remarkable effort. But there was too much monotony in the delivery of one or two lectures over and over, and his natural aversion to committed speeches induced Mr. Martin to quit the lecturing field. He now resolved to resume his studies, and for this purpose he removed to Detroit, Michigan, where he commenced under the tutorage of an able Baptist minister. Feeling that he was called to preach, soon after this he began the study of theology, and remained the student until his education was so far finished that he felt justified in his own mind to commence lecturing and preaching. About this time he made the tour of the State of Michigan, and lectured with great success. In the beautiful and flourishing town of Coldwater, he addressed a large and influential meeting, and the effect upon the audience was such as to raise the speaker high in their estimation. The weekly paper said of this lecture,--

"Our citizens filled the court house to hear J. S. Martin speak for his own race and in behalf of the oppressed. The citizens admired and were even astonished at his success as a public speaker. He is a natural orator, and, considering his opportunities, is one of the most interesting and forcible speakers of his age, and of the age. Indeed, he is a prodigy. It would seem impossible that one kept in 'chains and slavery,' and in total ignorance till within a few months, could so soon attain so vast a knowledge of the English language, and so clear and comprehensive a view of general subjects. Nature has made him a great man. His propositions and his arguments, his deductions and illustrations, are new and original; his voice and manner are at his command and prepossessing; his efforts are unstudied and effectual. The spirit which manifests itself is one broken loose from bondage and stimulated with freedom."

Shortly after this, Mr. Martin was ordained and settled over the Michigan Street Baptist Church, Buffalo, New York, where he labored with signal success till April, 1859, when he removed east. During the same summer he was introduced to the Boston public by Mr. Kalloch, the popular preacher at the Tremont Temple. The latter, pleased with Mr. Martin, secured his services while away on his annual vacation, which occupied six or eight weeks. No place of religious worship was more thronged than the Temple during the time that he filled its pulpit. At the termination of his engagement at the Temple, Mr. Martin was invited by Dr. Eddy to preach for him a few weeks, which be did with credit to himself and satisfaction to the society. The first Baptist Church at Lawrence being without a pastor, Mr. Martin was engaged to supply the pulpit, and was there seven or eight months, and might have remained longer; but during this time he received a call from the Joy Street Church, Boston, and feeling that his labor was more needed with his own color, he accepted the latter. He has now been at the Joy Street Church about three years, where his preaching has met with marked success. That society had long been in a declining state; but the church is now as well filled on Sundays as any place in the city. In the summer of 1861, Mr. Martin visited England, and remained abroad six months, where he did good service for the cause of freedom. On his return home he was warmly welcomed by his church and congregation. Soon after, he secured the freedom of his only sister and her two children, whom he settled at the west. In person, Mr. Martin is somewhat taller than the medium height; firm, dignified walk; not what would be termed handsome, but has a pleasing countenance; in race, half and half; eyes clear and bright; forehead well developed; gentlemanly in his deportment; has a popularity not surpassed by any of the preachers of Boston.

He has written considerable for the press, both prose and poetry. Some of the latter is much admired. His poem "The Hero and the Slave" has been read in public entertainments, and received with applause.

## CHARLES LENOX REMOND.

CHARLES L. REMOND is a native of Salem, Mass. He has the honor, we believe, of being the first colored man to take the field as a lecturer against slavery. He has been, more or less, in the employ of the Anti-Slavery Society for the past twenty-eight or thirty years. In 1840, he visited England has a delegate to the first "World's Anti-Slavery Convention," held in London. He remained abroad nearly two years, lecturing in the various towns and cities of Great Britain and Ireland. The following lines, addressed to him, appeared in one of the public journals, after the delivery of one of his thrilling speeches, in Belfast, and will give some idea of the estimation in which he was held as a platform speaker.
TO C. L. REMOND.

> Go forth and fear not! Glorious is the cause
> Which thou dost advocate; and nobly, too,
> Hast thou fulfilled thy mission--nobly raised
> Thy voice against oppression, and the woes

Of injured millions; and, if they are men,
Who can deny for them a Saviour died?
Nor will it e'er be asked, in that dread day
When black and white shall stand before the throne
Of Him their common Parent, "Unto which
Partition of the human race didst thou
Belong on earth?" Enough for thee to fill
The lot assigned thee, as ordained by Heaven.
I would not praise thee, Remond,--thou hast gifts
Bestowed upon thee for a noble end;
And for the use of which account must be
Returned to Him who lent them. May this thought
Preserve thee in his fear, and may the praise
Be given only to his mighty name.
And if, returning to thy native land,
By thee beloved, though dark with crimes that stain
Her boasted freedom, thou art called to prove
Thy true allegiance, even then go forth
Resigned to suffer,--trust thy all to Him
Who can support thee, whilst a still, small voice,
Within thy breast, shall whisper, "All is well."

Mr. Remond was welcomed on his return home, and again resumed his vocation as at lecturer. In stature he is small, spare made, neat, wiry build, and genteel in his personal appearance. He has a good voice, and is considered one of the best declaimers in New England. Faultless in his dress, and an excellent horseman, Mr. Remond has long been regarded the Count D'Orsay of the anti-slavery movement. He has written little or nothing for the press, and his notoriety is confined solely to the platform. Sensitive to a fault, and feeling sorely the prejudice against color which exists throughout the United States, his addresses have been mainly on that subject, on which he is always interesting. He is a good writer who embodies in his works the soul and spirit of the times in which he lives,--provided they are worth embodying,--and the common sympathy of the great mass is sounder criticism by far than the rules of mere scholars, who, buried up in their formulas, cannot speak so as to arrest the attention or move the heart. Adaptation without degeneracy is the great law to be followed. What is true of the writer is also true of the speaker. No man can put more real meaning in fewer words than Mr. Remond, and no one can give them greater force. The following extract from a speech of Mr. Remond, delivered before the New England Anti-Slavery Convention, at its anniversary in May, 1859, is characteristic of his style.

"If I had but one reason, why I consented to appear here, it was because, at this moment, I believe it belongs to the colored man in this country to say that his lot is a common one with every white man north of the Potomac River; and if you ask me who are my clients, I think I may answer, 'Every man north of Mason and Dixon's line, without reference to his complexion.' I have read in the newspapers that one or two distinguished men of this city propose to spend the coming summer in Europe. Born in Boston, educated at Harvard, having been dandled in the lap of Massachusetts favor and Massachusetts popularity, they are about to travel in Europe, among despotisms, monarchies, aristocracies, and oligarchies; and I trust in God they may learn, as they travel in those countries, that it is an everlasting disgrace that on the soil on which they were born, no man of color can stand and be considered free. If they shall learn no more than this, I will wish them a pleasant and prosperous tour; and unless they shall learn this, I hope they will come back and have the same padlock put upon their lips that is put upon men south of Mason and Dixon line.

"I want to ask this large audience, Mr. Chairman, through you, supposing the citizens of Boston should call a meeting to-morrow, and resolve that, in the event of a southern man, with southern principles, being elected to the presidential office, this state will secede, how would the State of Mississippi receive it? Now, I am here to ask that the non-slaveholding states shall dare to do, and write, and publish, and resolve, in behalf of freedom, as the slaveholders dare to act and resolve in behalf of slavery.

The time has been, Mr. Chairman, when a colored man could scarcely look a white man in the face without trembling, owing to his education and experience. I am not here to boast; but I may say, in view of what I have seen and heard during the last five years, as I said in the Representatives' Hall a few months ago, that our lot is a common one, and the sooner we shall so regard it, and buckle on our knapsacks and shoulder our muskets, and resolve that we will be free, the better for you as well as for me. The disgrace that once rested upon the head of the black man, now hovers over the head of every man and woman whom. I have the honor to address this evening, just in proportion as they shall dare to stand erect before the oligarchy of slaveholders in the southern portion of our country; and God hasten forward the day when not only Music Hall, but every other hall in the city of Boston, the Athens of America, shall be made eloquent with tones that shall speak, as man has never before spoken in this country, for the cause of universal freedom. If the result of that speaking must be bloodshed, be it so! If it must be the dissolution of the Union, be it so! If it must be that we must walk over or through the American church, he it so! The time has come when, if you value your own freedom, James Buchanan must be hung in effigy, and such men as Dr. Nehemiah Adams must be put in the pillory of public disgrace and contempt; and then Massachusetts will cease to be a hissing and a by-word in every other country."

## GEORGE T. DOWNING.

THE tall, fine figure, manly walk, striking profile, and piercing eye of George T. Downing would attract attention in any community, even where he is unknown. Possessing remarkable talents, finely educated, a keen observer, and devoted to the freedom and elevation of his race, he has long been looked upon as a representative man. A good debater, quick to take advantage of the weak points of an opponent, forcible in speech, and a natural orator, Mr. Downing is always admired as a speaker. Chosen president of the convention of colored citizens which assembled in Boston on the first of August, 1859, he delivered an impressive and eloquent opening address, of which we regret that we can give only an extract. He said,--

"The great consideration that presses upon me is, what may we do to make ourselves of more importance in community--necessary, indispensable? To sustain such a relation as this to community, (and it is possible,) is to secure, beyond a question, all the respect, to make sure the enjoyment of all the rights, that the most deferred to of the land enjoy. Society is deferential; it defers to power. Learning, and wealth, and power are most potent in society. It is not necessary that many men and women of us be wealthy and learned before we can force respect as a class; but it is necessary that we exhibit a proportionate representative character for learning and wealth, to be respected. It is not numbers alone, it is not universal wealth, it is not general learning, that secures to those, known by a distinction in society as whites--that gains them power; for they are not generally wealthy, not commonly learned. The number of these among them, as in all communities, is limited; but that number forms a representative character, some of whom excel; hence they have power--the class enjoy a name.

"There is another sense of power in community, which, though silent, has its weight--it should be most potent: that power is moral character. This also, like the other powers of which I have spoken, need not be universal to have an effect favorable to a class. I think that I am not claiming too much for the colored people in asserting that we have a decent representation in this respect--a most remarkable one, considering all the depressing influences which the present and preceding generations have had to struggle up under. Happily, this power on community is not growing less; it is on the increase. An illustration of the correctness of my position as to the power of a representative character for wealth and learning in commanding respect, is forcibly exhibited in the Celts in our midst, who came among us poor and ignorant, and who, consequently, fill menial, dependent positions. They are the least respected of all immigrants. In speaking thus, I am simply dealing with facts, not intending to be invidious. The German element, mingling with the general element which comes among us, representing a higher intelligence, more wealth, with great practical industry, is silently stealing a hold, a power in the nation, because of these possessions, at which native America will yet start. Now, gentlemen, if these be the facts, is it not well for us, as sensible men here assembled, to consider our best interest--to have in view these sources of power? Would it not be well to consider these--to fall upon some plan by which we may possess or excite to the possession of them--rather than devote much of our time in a discussion as to the injustice of our fellow-countrymen in their relation to us? Of this they know full well, and we too bitterly.

"The ballot is a power in this country which should not be lost sight of by us. Were it more generally exercised by the colored people, the effect would be very perceptible. Those of them residents of the states that deny them the privilege of the elective franchise, should earnestly strive to have the right and the power secured to them; those who have it should never let an occasion pass, when they may consistently exercise it, without doing so. We know that the government and the states have acted most unfairly in their relation to us; but that government and the states, in doing so, have clearly disregarded justice, as well as perverted the legal interpretation of the supreme law of the land, as set forth in its constitution; which facts alone require that we exercise the right to vote, whenever we can, towards correcting this injustice. Were it known on election day that any colored man would deposit a vote, that there would be a concert of action doing so, the effect would be irresistible. Cannot a vote be cast at the approaching presidential election? Will the Republican party (a party which is entitled to credit for the service it has rendered to the cause of freedom) put in nomination, in 1860, for whom we can, with some degree of consistency, cast our ballots? It has such men in its ranks--prominent men of the party--men who are available.

"I would have it noted, that we cannot vote for a man who subscribes to the doctrine that, in struggling for freedom in a presidential or any other election, he ignores the rights of the colored man.

"There is all increased as well as an increasing respect for us in community. This is not simply because we have friends (all praise to them) who speak out boldly and uncompromisingly for the right,--in fact, the most of their efforts have been directed towards relieving the country of the blight and of the injustice of slavery,--but it is because our character, as a class, is better understood."

Mr. Downing is a native of New York, but spends his summers at Newport, where he has an excellent retreat for those seeking that fashionable watering-place, and where he stands high with the better class of the community.

## ROBERT PURVIS.

FEW private gentlemen are better known than Robert Purvis. Born in Charleston, S. C., a son of the late venerable William Purvis, Esq., educated in Now England, and early associated with William Lloyd Garrison, Francis Jackson, and Wendell Phillips, he has always been understood as belonging to the most ultra wing of the radical abolitionists. Residing in Philadelphia when it was unsafe to avow one's self a friend of the slave, Mr. Purvis never was known to deny his hatred to the "peculiar institution." A writer for one of the public journals, seeking out distinguished colored persons as subjects for his pen, paid him a visit, of which the following is his account:--

"The stage put us down at his gate, and we were warned to be ready to return in an hour and a half. His dwelling stands some distance back from the turnpike. It is approached by a broad lawn, and shaded with ancient trees. In the rear stands a fine series of barns. There are magnificent orchards connected with his farm, and his live stock is of the most approved breeds. We understand that he receives numbers of premiums annually from agricultural societies. In this fine old mansion Mr. Purvis has resided many years.

"We were ushered, upon our visit, into a pleasant dining room, hung with a number of paintings. Upon one side of an old-fashioned mantel was a large portrait of a fine looking white man; on the other side, a portrait of a swarthy negro. Above these old John Brown looked gloomily down like a bearded patriarch.

"In a few minutes Mr. Purvis came in. We had anticipated a stubborn-looking negro, with a swagger, and a tone of bravado. In place of such we saw a tall, beautifully knit gentleman, almost white, and handsomely dressed. His foot and hand were symmetrical and, although his hair was gray with years, every limb was full, and every movement supple and easy. He saluted us with decorous dignity, and began to converse.

"It was difficult to forget that the man before us was not of our own race. The topics upon which he spoke were chiefly personal. He related some very amusing anecdotes of his relations with southern gentlemen. On, one occasion he applied for a passage to Liverpool in a Philadelphia packet. Some southern gentlemen, unacquainted with Purvis, save as a man of negro blood, protested that he should not be received. Among these was a Mr. Hayne, a near relative of Hayne the orator.

"Purvis accordingly went to Liverpool by another vessel. He met Hayne and the southerners as they were about returning home, and took passage with them, passing for a white man. He gained their esteem, was cordially invited by each to visit him in the south, and no entertainment was complete without his joke and his presence. At a final dinner, given to the party by the captain of the vessel, Mr. Hayne, who had all along spoken violently of the negro race, publicly toasted Mr. Purvis, as the finest type of the Caucasian race he had ever met.

"Mr. Purvis rose to reply. 'I am not a Caucasian,' said he; 'I belong to the degraded tribe of Africans.'

The feelings of the South Carolinians need not be described.

"Mr. Purvis has written a number of anti-slavery pamphlets, and is regarded, by rumor, as the president of the Underground Railroad. He has figured in many slave-rescue cases, some of which he relates with graphic manner of description.

"He is the heaviest tax-payer in the township, and owns two very valuable farms. By his influence the public schools of the township have been thrown open to colored children. He has also built, at his own expense, a hall for free debate. We left him with feelings of higher regard than we have yet felt for any of his people. It is proper to remark, that Purvis is the grandchild of a blackamoor, who was taken a slave to South Carolina."

Although disdaining all profession of a public character, Mr. Purvis is, nevertheless, often invited to address public gatherings. As a speaker he is energetic, eloquent, and sarcastic. He spares neither friend nor foe in his argument; uses choice language, and appears to feel that nature and humanity are the everlasting proprietors of truth, and that truth should be spoken at all times. Mr. Purvis is an able writer, and whatever he says comes directly from the heart. His letter to Hon. S. C. Pomeroy, on colonization, is characteristic of him. We regret that space will not allow us to give the whole of this timely and manly production.

"There are some aspects of this project which surely its advocates cannot have duly considered. You purpose to exile hundreds and thousands of your laborers. The wealth of a country consists mainly in its labor. With what law of economy, political or social, can you reconcile this project to banish from your shores the men that plough your fields, drive your teams, and help build your houses? Already the farmers around me begin to feel the pinching want of labor; how will it be after this enormous draft? I confess the project seems to me one of insanity. What will foreign nations, on whose good or ill will so much is supposed now to depend, think of this project? These nations have none of this vulgar prejudice against complexion. what, then, will they think of the wisdom of a people who, to gratify a low-born prejudice, deliberately plan to drive out hundreds and thousands of the most peaceful, industrious, and competent laborers? Mr. Roebuck said in a late speech at Sheffield, as an argument for intervention, 'that the feeling against the black was stronger at the north than in the south.' Mr. Roebuck can now repeat that assertion, and point to this governmental project in corroboration of its truth. A 'Slaveholders' Convention' was held a few years since in Maryland to consider whether it would not be best either to re-enslave the free blacks of that state, or banish them from its borders. The question was discussed, and a committee, the chairman of which was United States Senator Pearce, was appointed to report upon it. That committee reported 'that to enslave men now free would be inhuman, and to banish them from the state would be to inflict a deadly blow upon the material interests of the commonwealth; that their labor was indispensable to the welfare of the state.' Sir, your government proposes to do that which the Slaveholders' Convention of Maryland, with all their hate of the free blacks, declared to be inconsistent with the public interest.

But it is said this is a question of prejudice, of national antipathy, and not to be reasoned about. The President has said, 'whether it is right or wrong I need not now discuss.'

"Great God! Is justice nothing? Is honor nothing? Is even pecuniary interest to be sacrificed to this insane and vulgar hate? But it is said this is the 'white Man's country.' Not so, sir. This is the red man's country by natural right, and the black man's by virtue of his sufferings and toil. Your fathers by violence drove the red man out, and forced the black man in. The children of the black man have enriched the soil by their tears, and sweat, and blood. Sir, we were born here, and here we choose to remain. For twenty years we were goaded and harassed by systematic efforts to make us colonize. We were coaxed and mobbed, and mobbed and coaxed, but we refused to budge. We planted ourselves upon our inalienable rights, and were proof against all the efforts that were made to expatriate us. For the last fifteen years we have enjoyed comparative quiet. Now again the malign project is broached, and again, as before, in the name of humanity are we invited to leave.

"In God's name, what good do you expect to accomplish by such a course? If you will not let our brethren in bonds go free, if you will not let us, as did our fathers, share in the privileges of the government, if you will not let us even help fight the battles of the country, in Heaven's name, at least, let us alone. Is that too great a boon to ask of your magnanimity?

"I elect to stay on the soil on which I was born, and on the plot of ground which I have fairly bought and honestly paid for. Don't advise me to leave, and don't add insult to injury by telling me it's for my own good; of that I am to be the judge. It is in vain that you talk to me about the 'two races,' and their 'mutual antagonism.' In the matter of rights there is but one race, and that is the human race. 'God has made of one blood all nations to dwell on all the face of the earth.' And it is not true that there is a mutual antagonism between the white and colored people of this community.

You may antagonize us, but we do not antagonize you. You may hate us, but we do not hate you. It may argue a want of spirit to cling to those who seek to banish us, but such is, nevertheless, the fact.

"Sir, this is our country as much as it is yours, and we will not leave it. Your ships may be at the door, but we choose to remain. A few may go, as a few went to Hayti, and a few to Liberia; but the colored people as a mass will not leave the land of their birth. Of course, I can only speak by authority for myself; but I know the people with whom I am identified, and I feel confident that I only express their sentiment as a body when I say that your project of colonizing them in Central America, or any where else, with or without their consent, will never succeed. They will migrate, as do other people, when left to themselves, and when the motive is sufficient; but they will neither be 'compelled to volunteer,' nor constrained to go of their 'own accord.'"

# JOSEPH JENKINS.

"Look here, upon this picture, and on this."-- HAMLET.

No one accustomed to pass through Cheapside could fail to have noticed a good-looking man, neither black nor white, engaged in distributing bills to the thousands who throng that part of the city of London. While strolling through Cheapside, one morning, I saw, for the fiftieth time, Joseph Jenkins, the subject of this article, handing out his bills to all who would take them as he thrust them into their hands. I confess that I was not a little amused, and stood for some moments watching and admiring his energy in distributing his papers. A few days after, I saw the same individual in Chelsea, sweeping a crossing; here, too, he was equally as energetic as when I met him in the city. Some days later, while going through Kensington, I heard rather a sweet, musical voice singing a familiar psalm, and on looking round was not a little surprised to find that it was the Cheapside bill-distributor and Chelsea crossing-sweeper. He was now singing hymns, and selling religious tracts. I am fond of patronizing genius, and therefore took one of his tracts and paid him for a dozen.

During the following week, I saw, while going up the City Road, that Shakspeare's tragedy of Othello was to be performed at the Eagle Saloon that night, and that the character of the Moor was to be taken by "Selim, an African prince." Having no engagement that evening, I resolved at once to attend, to witness the performance of the "African Talma," as he was called. It was the same interest that had induced me to go to the Italian opera to see Mesdames Sontag and Grisi in Norma, and to visit Drury Lane to see Macready take leave of the stage. My expectations were screwed up to the highest point. The excitement caused by the publication of "Uncle Tom's Cabin" had prepared the public for any thing in the African line, and I felt that the prince would be sure of a good audience; and in this I was not disappointed, for, as I took my seat in one of the boxes near the stage, I saw that the house was crammed with an orderly company. The curtain was already up when I entered, and Iago and Roderigo were on the stage.

After a while Othello came in, and was greeted with thunders of applause, which he very gracefully acknowledged. Just black enough to take his part without coloring his face, and being tall, with a good figure and all easy carriage, a fine, full, and musical voice, he was well adapted to the character of Othello. I immediately recognized in the countenance of the Moor a face that I had seen before, but could not at the moment tell where. Who could this "prince" be? thought I. He was too black for Douglass, not black enough for Ward, not tall enough for Garnet, too calm for Delany, figure, though fine, not genteel enough for Remond. However, I was soon satisfied as to who the star was. Reader, would you think it? it was no less a person than Mr. Jenkins, the bill-distributor from Cheapside, and crossing-sweeper from Chelsea! For my own part, I was overwhelmed with amazement, and it was some time before I could realize the fact. He soon showed that he possessed great dramatic power and skill; and his description to the Senate of how he won the affections of the gentle Desdemona stamped him at once as an actor of merit. "What a pity," said a lady near me to a gentleman that was by her side, "that a prince of the royal blood of Africa should have to go upon the stage for a living! It is indeed a shame!" When he came to the scene,--

> "O, cursed, cursed slave!--whip me, ye devils,
> From the possession of this heavenly sight!
> Blow me about in winds, roast me in sulphur!
> Wash me in steep-down gulfs of liquid fire!
> O, Desdemona! Desdemona! dead?
> Dead? O! O! O!"--

the effect was indeed grand. When the curtain fell, the prince was called upon the stage, where he was received with deafening shouts of approbation, and a number of bouquets thrown at his feet, which he picked up, bowed, and retired. I went into Cheapside the next morning, at an early hour, to see if the prince had given up his old trade for what I supposed to be a more lucrative one; but I found the hero of the previous night at his post, and giving out his bills as energetically as when I had last seen him. Having to go to the provinces for some months, I lost sight of Mr. Jenkins, and on my return to town did not trouble myself to look him up. More than a year after I had witnessed the representation of Othello at the Eagle, I was walking, one pleasant Sabbath evening, through one of the small streets in the borough, when I found myself in front of a little chapel, where a number of persons were going in. As I was passing on slowly, an elderly man said to me, "I suppose you have come to hear your colored brother preach." "No," I answered; "I was not aware that one was to be here." "Yes," said he; "and a clever man he is, too." As the old man offered to find me a seat, I concluded to go in and hear this son of Africa. The room, which was not large, was already full. I had to wait but a short time before the reverend gentleman made his appearance. He was nearly black, and dressed in a black suit, with high shirt-collar, and an intellectual-looking cravat, that nearly hid his chin. A pair of spectacles covered his eyes. The preacher commenced by reading a portion of Scripture, and then announced that they would sing the twenty-eighth hymn in "the arrangement." O, that voice! I felt sure that I had heard that musical voice before; but where, I could not tell. I was not aware that any of my countrymen were in London, but felt that, whoever he was, he was no discredit to the race; for he was a most eloquent and accomplished orator. His sermon was against the sale and use of intoxicating drinks, and the bad habits of the working classes, of whom his audience was composed.

Although the subject was intensely interesting, I was impatient for it to come to a close, for I wanted to speak to the preacher. But the evening being warm, and the room heated, the reverend gentleman, on wiping the perspiration from his face, (which, by the way, ran very freely,) took off his spectacles on one occasion, so that I immediately recognized him, which saved me from going up to the pulpit at the end of the service. Yes; it was the bill-distributor of Cheapside, the crossing-sweeper of Chelsea, the tract-seller and psalm-singer of Kensington, and the Othello of the Eagle Saloon. I could scarcely keep from laughing outright when I discovered this to be the man that I had seen in so many characters. As I was about leaving my seat at the close of the services, the old man who showed me into the chapel asked me if I would not like to be introduced to the minister; and I immediately replied that I would. We proceeded up the aisle, and met the clergyman as he was descending. On seeing me, he did not wait for a formal introduction, but put out his hand and said, "I have seen you so often, sir, that I seem to know you." "Yes," I replied; "we have met several times, and under different circumstances." Without saying more, he invited me to walk with him towards his home, which was in the direction of my own residence. We proceeded; and, during the walk, Mr. Jenkins gave me some little account of his early history. "You think me rather an odd fish, I presume," said he. "Yes," I replied. "You are not the only one who thinks so," continued he. "Although I am not as black as some of my countrymen, I am a native of Africa. Surrounded by some beautiful mountain scenery, and situated between Darfour and Abyssinia, two thousand miles in the interior of Africa, is a small valley going by the name of Tegla. To that valley I stretch forth my affections, giving it the endearing appellation of my native home and fatherland. It was there that I was born, it was there that I received the fond looks of a loving mother, and it was there that I set my feet, for the first time, upon a world full of cares, trials, difficulties, and dangers. My father being a farmer, I used to be sent out to take care of his goats. This service I did when I was between seven and eight years of age. As I was the eldest of the boys, my pride was raised in no small degree when I beheld my father preparing a farm for me. This event filled my mind with the grand anticipation of leaving the care of the goats to my brother, who was then beginning to work a little. While my father was making these preparations, I had the constant charge of the goats; and being accompanied by two other boys, who resided near my father's house, we wandered many miles from home, by which means we acquired a knowledge of the different districts of our country.

It was while in these rambles with my companions that I became the victim of the slave-trader. We were tied with cords and taken to Tegla, and thence to Kordofan, which is under the jurisdiction of the Pacha of Egypt. From Kordofan I was brought down to Dongola and Korti, in Nubia, and from thence down the Nile to Cairo; and, after being sold nine times, I became the property of an English gentleman, who brought me to this country and put me into school. But he died before I finished my education, and his family feeling no interest in me, I had to seek a living as best I could. I have been employed for some years to distribute handbills for a barber in Cheapside in the morning, go to Chelsea and sweep a crossing in the afternoon, and sing psalms and sell religious tracts in the evening. Sometimes I have an engagement to perform at some of the small theatres, as I had when you saw me at the Eagle. I preach for this little congregation over here, and charge them nothing; for I want that the poor should have the gospel without money and without price. I have now given up distributing bills; I have settled my son in that office. My eldest daughter was married about three months ago; and I have presented her husband with the Chelsea crossing, as my daughter's wedding portion." "Can he make a living at it?" I eagerly inquired. "O, yes; that crossing at Chelsea is worth thirty shillings a week, if it is well swept," said he. "But what do you do for a living for yourself?" I asked. "I am the leader of a band," he continued; "and we play for balls and parties, and three times a week at the Holborn Casino." "You are determined to rise," said I. "Yes," he replied,--

> 'Upward, onward, is my watchword;
> Though the winds blow good or ill,
> Though the sky be fair or stormy,
> This shall be my watchword still,'"

By this time we had reached a point where we had to part; and I left Joseph Jenkins, impressed with the idea that he was the greatest genius that I had met in Europe.

# JOHN S. ROCK.

THE subject of this sketch was born in Salem, N. J., in 1825. When quite a child, he became passionately attached to his book, and, unlike most children, seldom indulged in amusements of any kind. His parents, anxious to make the most of his talents, kept him at school until he was eighteen years of age, at which time he was examined and approved as a teacher of public schools. He taught school from 1844 to 1848. Mr. David Allen writes, "His was certainly the most orderly, and the best conducted, school I ever visited, although myself a teacher for nearly twenty years." During the time Mr. Rock was teaching, Drs. Sharp and Gibbon opened their libraries to him, and he commenced the study of physic,--teaching six hours, studying eight, and giving private lessons two hours every day. After completing his medical studies, he found it impossible to get into a medical college; so he abandoned his idea of becoming a physician, and went with Dr. Harbert and studied dentistry. He finished his studies in the summer of 1849. In January, 1850, he went to Philadelphia to practise his profession. In 1851, he received a silver medal for artificial teeth. In the same year, he took a silver medal for a prize essay on temperance. After the Apprentices' High School had been established in Philadelphia, and while it was still an evening school, Mr. Rock took charge of it, and kept it until it was merged into a day school, under the direction of Professor Reason. He attended lectures in the American Medical College, and graduated in 1852.

In 1853, Dr. Rock came to Boston, where he now resides. On leaving the city of Philadelphia, the professors of the Dental College gave him letters bearing testimony to his high professional skill and integrity. Professor Townsend writes, "Dr. Rock is a graduate of a medical school in this city, and is favorably known, and much respected, by the profession. Having seen him operate, it gives me great pleasure to bear my testimony to his superior abilities." Professor J. F. B. Flagg writes, "I have seen his operations, and have been much pleased with them. As a scientific man, I shall miss the intercourse which I have so long enjoyed in his acquaintance." After Mr. R. graduated in medicine, he practised both of his professions. In 1856, he accepted an invitation to deliver a lecture on the "Unity of the Human Races," before the Massachusetts legislature. In 1857, he delivered the oration on the occasion of the dedication of the new Masonic Temple in Eleventh Street, Philadelphia. His intense application to study and to business had so undermined his health that, in the summer of 1856, he was obliged to give up all business. After several unsuccessful surgical operations here, and when nearly all hope for the restoration of his health was gone, he determined to go to France. When he was ready to go, he applied to the government for a passport. This was refused, Mr. Cass, then secretary of state, saying in reply, that "a passport had never been granted to a colored man since the foundation of the government." Mr. Rock went to France, however, and underwent a severe surgical operation at the hands of the celebrated Nélaton. Professor Nélaton advised him to give up dentistry altogether; and as his shattered Constitution forbade the exposure necessary for the practice of medicine, he gave up both, and bent all his energies to the study of law. In 1860, he accepted an invitation, and delivered a lecture on the "Character and Writings of Madame De Staël," before the Massachusetts legislature which he did "with credit to himself and satisfaction, to the very large audience in attendance." Der Pionier, a German newspaper, in Boston, said when commenting on his criticism of De Staël's "Germany," "This thinking, educated German and French speaking negro proved himself as learned in German as he is in French literature." On the 14th of September, 1861, on motion of T. K. Lothrop, Esq., Dr. Rock was examined in the Superior Court, before Judge Russell, and admitted to practice as an attorney and counsellor at law in all the courts of Massachusetts. On the 21st of the same month Mr. Rock received a commission from the governor and council as a justice of the peace for seven years for the city of Boston and county of Suffolk.

We annex an extract from a speech made by him before the last anniversary of the Massachusetts Anti-Slavery Society.

"Other countries are held out as homes for us. Why is this? Why is it that the people from all other countries are invited to come here, and we are asked to go away? Is it to make room for the refuse population of Europe? Or why is it that the white people of this country desire to get rid of us? Does any one pretend to deny that this is our country? or that much of its wealth and prosperity is the result of the labor of our hands? or that our blood and bones have crimsoned and whitened every battle-field from Maine to Louisiana? Why this desire to get rid of us? Can it be possible that because the nation has robbed us for more than two centuries, and now finds that she can do it no longer and preserve a good character among the nations, she, out of hatred, wishes to banish, because she cannot continue to rob, us? Or why is it? I will tell you. The free people of color have succeeded in spite of every thing; and we are today a living refutation of that shameless assertion that we cannot take care of ourselves. Abject as our condition has been, our whole lives prove us to be superior to the influences that have been brought to bear upon us to crush us. This cannot be said of your race when it was oppressed and enslaved. Another reason is, this nation has wronged us; therefore many hate us. The Spanish proverb is, 'Since I have wronged you I have never liked you.' This is true of every class of people. When a man wrongs another, he not only hates him, but tries to make others dislike him. Unnatural as this may appear, it is nevertheless true. You may help a man during his lifetime, and he will speak well of you; but your first refusal will incur his displeasure, and show you his ingratitude. When he has got all he can from you, he has no further use for you. When the orange is squeezed, we throw it aside. The black man is a good fellow while he is a slave, and toils for nothing; but the moment he claims his own flesh and blood and bones, he is a most obnoxious creature, and there is a proposition to get rid of him. He is happy while he remains, a poor, degraded, ignorant slave, without even the right to his own offspring. While in this condition the master can ride in the same carriage, sleep in the same bed, and nurse from the same bosom. But give this slave the right to use his own legs, his hands, his body, and his mind, and this happy and desirable creature is instantly transformed into a most loathsome wretch, fit only to be colonized somewhere near the mountains of the moon, or eternally banished from civilized beings! You must not lose sight of the fact it is the emancipated slave and the free colored man that it is proposed to remove-- not the slave. This country is perfectly adapted to negro slavery; it is the free blacks that the air is not good for! What an idea! a country good for slavery and not good for freedom! This monstrous idea would be scorned by even a Fejee Islander."

As a public speaker Mr. Rock stands deservedly high; his discourses being generally of an elevated tone, and logically put together. As a member of the Boston bar, he has thus far succeeded well, and bids fair to obtain his share of public patronage. In personal appearance Mr. Rock is tall and of good figure, with a thoughtful countenance and a look that indicates the student. In color he is what is termed a grief, about one remove from the negro. By his own color he has long been regarded as a representative man.

## WILLIAM DOUGLASS.

WILLIAM DOUGLASS was a clergyman of the Protestant Episcopal denomination, and for a number of years was rector of St. Thomas Church, Philadelphia. We met Mr. Douglass in England in 1852, and became impressed with the belief that he was no ordinary man. He had a finished education, being well versed in Latin, Greek, and Hebrew. He possessed large and philanthropic views, but was extremely diffident, which gave one the opinion that he was a man of small ability. Being in Philadelphia in the spring of 1860, we attended the morning service at his church. When the preacher made his appearance, all eyes were turned to the pulpit. His figure was prepossessing--a great thing in a public speaker. Weak, stunted, deformed-looking men labor under much disadvantage. Mr. Douglass had a commanding look, a clear, musical voice, and was a splendid reader. He was no dull drone when the service was over and the sermon had commenced. With downcast eye he read no moral essay that touched no conscience and fired no heart. On the contrary, he was spirited in the pulpit. He looked his congregation in the face; he directed his discourse to them. He took care that not a single word should lose its aim. No one fell asleep while he was speaking, but all seemed intensely interested in the subject in hand. Mr. Douglass was a general favorite with the people of his own city, and especially, the members of his society. He was a talented writer, and published, a few years ago, a volume of sermons,which are filled with gems of thought and original ideas. A feeling of deep piety and humanity runs through the entire book. Mr. Douglass was of unmixed blood, gentlemanly in his manners, chaste in conversation, and social in private life. Though not active in public affairs, he was, nevertheless, interested in all that concerned the freedom and elevation of his race. He visited England and the West Indies some years ago, and had an extensive acquaintance beyond the limits of his own country. Mr. Douglass was respected and esteemed by the white clergy of Philadelphia, who were forced to acknowledge his splendid abilities.

## ELYMAS PAYSON ROGERS.

E. P. ROGERS, a clergyman of the Presbyterian order, and pastor of a church at Newark, New Jersey, was a man of education, research, and literary ability. He was not a fluent and easy speaker, but he was logical, and spoke with a degree of refinement seldom met with. He possessed poetical genius of no mean order, and his poem on the "Missouri Compromise," which he read in many of the New England cities and towns in 1856, contains brilliant thoughts and amusing suggestions. The following on Truth is not without point:--

"When Truth is girded for the fight,
And draws her weapons keen and bright,
And lifts aloft her burnished shield,
Her godlike influence to wield,

If victory in that self-same hour
Is not accomplished by her power,
She'll not retreat nor flee away,
But win the field another day.
She will with majesty arise,
Seize her traducers by surprise,
And by her overwhelming might

Will put her deadly foes to flight."

The allusion to the threat of the south against the north is a happy one, in connection with the rebellion.

"I'll show my power the country through,
And will the factious north subdue;
And Massachusetts shall obey,
And yield to my increasing sway.
She counts her patriotic deeds,
But scatters her disunion seeds;
She proudly tells us of the tea
Sunk by her worthies in the sea,
And then she talks more proudly still
Of Lexington and Bunker Hill;
But on that hill, o'er patriots' graves,
I'll yet enroll my negro slaves.
I may have trouble, it is true,
But still I'll put the rebels through,
And make her statesmen bow the knee,
Yield to my claims, and honor me.
And though among them I shall find
The learned, the brilliant, and refined,
If on me they shall e'er reflect,
No senate chamber shall protect
Their guilty pates and heated brains,
From hideous gutta percha canes."

The election of N. P. Banks, as speaker of the House of Representatives, is mentioned in the succeeding lines:--

"But recently the north drove back
The southern tyrants from the track,
And put to flight their boasting ranks,
And gave the speaker's chair to Banks."

Mr. Rogers was of unmixed race, genteel in appearance, forehead large and well developed, fine figure, and pleasing in his manners. Anxious to benefit his race, he visited Africa in 1861, was attacked with the fever, and died in a few days. No man was more respected by all classes than he. His genial influence did much to soften down the pro-slavery feeling which existed in the city where he resided.

# J. THEODORE HOLLY.

IF there is any man living who is more devoted to the idea of a "Negro Nationality" than Dr. Delany, that man is J. Theodore Holly. Possessing a good education, a retentive memory, and being of studious habits, Mr. Holly has brought himself up to a point of culture not often attained by men even in the higher walks of life. Unadulterated in race, devotedly attached to Africa and her descendants, he has made a "Negro Nationality " a matter of much thought and study. He paid a visit to Hayti in 1858 or 1859, returned home, and afterwards preached, lectured, and wrote in favor of Haytian emigration. In concluding a long essay on this subject, in the Anglo-African Magazine, he says,--

"From these thoughts it will be seen that whatsoever is to be the future destiny of the descendants of Africa, Hayti certainly holds the most important relation to that destiny. And if we were to be reduced to the dread alternative of having her historic fame blotted out of existence, or that celebrity which may have been acquired elsewhere by all the rest of our race combined, we should say, Preserve the name, the fame, and the sovereign existence of Hayti, though every thing else shall perish. Yes, let Britain and France undermine, if they will, the enfranchisement which they gave to their West Indian slaves, by their present apprenticeship system; let the lone star of Liberia, placed in the firmament of nationalities by a questionable system of American philanthropy, go out in darkness; let the opening resources of Central Africa be again shut up in their wonted seclusion; let the names and deeds of our Nat Turners, Denmark Veseys, Penningtons, Delanys, Douglasses, and Smiths be forgotten forever; but never let the self-emancipating deeds of the Haytian people be effaced; never let her heroically achieved nationality be brought low; no, never let the names of her Toussaint, her Dessalines, her Rigaud, her Christophe, and her Petion be forgotten, or blotted out from the historic pages of the world's history."

Mr. Holly is a clergyman of the Protestant Episcopal order, and for several years was pastor of a church at New Haven, Connecticut, where he sustained the reputation of being an interesting and eloquent preacher.

His reading is at times rapid, yet clear and emphatic. He seems to aim more at what he says than how he says it; and if you listen, you will find food for thought in every phrase. As a writer he is forcible and argumentative, but never dull. In person, Mr. Holly is of the ordinary size, has a bright eye, agreeable countenance, form erect, voice clear and mellow. He uses good language, is precise in his manners, and wears the air of a gentleman. Infatuated with the idea of a home in Hayti, he raised a colony and sailed for Port au Prince in the spring of 1861. He was unfortunate in the selection of a location, and the most of those who went out with him, including his own family, died during their first six months on the island. Mr. Holly has recently returned to the United States. Whether he intends to remain or not, we are not informed.

# JAMES W. C. PENNINGTON.

DR. PENNINGTON was born a slave on the farm of Colonel Gordon, in the State of Maryland. His early life was not unlike the common lot of the bondmen of the Middle States. He was by trade a blacksmith, which increased his value to his owner. He had no opportunities for learning, and was ignorant of letters when he made his escape to the north. Through intense application to books, he gained, as far as it was possible, what slavery had deprived him of in his younger days. But he always felt the early blight upon his soul.

Dr. Pennington had not been free long ere he turned his attention to theology, and became an efficient preacher in the Presbyterian denomination. He was several years settled over a church at Hartford, Conn. He has been in Europe three times, his second visit being the most important, as he remained there three or four years, preaching and lecturing, during which time he attended the Peace Congresses held at Paris, Brussels, and London. While in Germany, the degree of Doctor of Divinity was conferred upon him by the University of Heidelberg. On his return to the United States be received a call, and was settled as pastor over Shiloh Church, New York city.

The doctor has been a good student, is a ripe scholar, and is deeply versed in theology. While at Paris, in 1849, we, with the American and English delegates to the Peace Congress, attended divine service at the Protestant Church, where Dr. Pennington had been invited to preach. His sermon on that occasion was an eloquent production, made a marked impression on his hearers, and created upon the minds of all a more elevated idea of the abilities of the negro. In past years he has labored zealously and successfully for the education and moral, social, and religious elevation of his race. The doctor is unadulterated in blood, with strongly-marked African features; in stature he is of the common size, slightly inclined to corpulency, with an athletic frame and a good constitution. The fact that Dr. Pennington is considered a good Greek, Latin, and German scholar, although his early life was spent in slavery, is not more strange than that Henry Diaz, the black commander in Brazil, is extolled in all the histories of that country as one of the most sagacious and talented men and experienced officers of whom they could boast; nor that Hannibal, an African,gained by his own exertion a goof education, and rose to be a lieutenant-general and director of artillery under Peter the Great; nor that Don Juan Latino, a negro, became teacher of the Latin language at Seville; nor that Anthony William Am, a native of Guinea, took the degree of Doctor of Philosophy at the University of Wittemburg; nor that James J. Capetein, fresh from the coast of Africa, became master of the Latin, Greek, Hebrew, and Chaldaic languages; nor that James Derham, an imported negro, should, by his own genius and energy, be considered one of the ablest physicians in New Orleans, and of whom Dr. Rush says, "I found him very learned. I thought I could give him information concerning the treatment of diseases; but I learned more from him than he could expect from me." We might easily extend the catalogue, for we have abundant materials. Blumenbach boldly affirms of the negro, "There is no savage people who have distinguished themselves by such examples of perfectibility and capacity for scientific cultivation."

## A MAN WITHOUT A NAME.

IT was in the month of December, 1852, while Colonel Rice and family were seated around a bright wood fire, whose blaze lighted up the large dining room in their old mansion, situated ten miles from Dayton, in the State of Ohio, that they heard a knock at the door, which was answered by the familiar "Come in" that always greets the stranger in the Western States. Squire Loomis walked in and took a seat on one of the three rocking-chairs, which had been made vacant by the young folks, who rose to give place to their highly influential and wealthy neighbor. It was a beautiful night; the sky was clear, the wind had bushed its deep moanings, the most brilliant of the starry throng stood out in bold relief, despite the superior light of the moon. "I see some one standing at the gate," said Mrs. Rice, as she left the window and came nearer the fire. "I'll go out and see who it is," exclaimed George, as he quitted his chair and started for the door. The latter soon returned and whispered to his father, and both left the room, evincing that something unusual was at hand. Not many minutes elapsed, however, before the father and son entered, accompanied by a young man, whose complexion showed plainly that other than Anglo-Saxon blood coursed through his veins. The whole company rose, and the stranger was invited to draw near to the fire. Question after question was now pressed upon the new-comer by the colonel and the squire, but without eliciting satisfactory replies.

"You need not be afraid, my friend," said the host, as he looked intently in the colored man's face, "to tell where you are from and to what place you are going. If you are a fugitive, as I suspect, give us your story, and we will protect and defend you to the last."

Taking courage from these kind remarks, the mulatto said, "I was born, sir, in the State of Kentucky, and raised in Missouri. My master was my father; my mother was his slave. That, sir, accounts for the fairness of my complexion. As soon as I was old enough to labor I was taken into my master's dwelling as a servant, to attend upon the family. My mistress, aware of my near relationship to her husband, felt humiliated, and often in her anger would punish me severely for no cause whatever. My near approach to the Anglo-Saxon aroused the jealousy and hatred of the overseer, and he flogged me, as he said, to make me know my place. My fellow-slaves hated me because I was whiter than themselves. Thus my complexion was construed into a crime, and I was made to curse my father for the Anglo-Saxon blood that courses through my veins.

"My master raised slaves to supply the southern market, and every year some of my companions were sold to the slave-traders and taken farther south. Husbands were separated from their wives, and children torn from the arms of their agonizing mothers. These outrages were committed by the man whom nature compelled me to look upon as my father. My mother and brothers were sold and taken away from me; still I bore all, and made no attempt to escape, for I yet had near me an only sister, whom I dearly loved. At last, the negro driver attempted to rob my sister of her virtue. She appealed to me for protection. Her innocence, beauty, and tears were enough to stir the stoutest heart. My own, filled with grief and indignation, swelled within me as though it would burst or leap from my bosom. My tears refused to flow: the fever in my brain dried them up. I could stand it no longer. I seized the wretch by the throat, and hurled him to the ground; and with this strong arm I paid him for old and new. The next day I was tried by a jury of slaveholders for the crime of having within me the heart of a man, and protecting my sister from the licentious embrace of a libertine. And-- would you believe it, sir?--that jury of enlightened Americans,--yes, sir, Christian Americans,- -after grave deliberation, decided that I had broken the laws, and sentenced me to receive five hundred lashes upon my bare back. But, sir, I escaped from them the night before I was to have been flogged.

"Afraid of being arrested and taken back, I remained the following day hid away in a secluded spot on the banks of the Mississippi River, protected from the gaze of man by the large trees and thick canebrakes that sheltered me. I waited for the coming of another night. All was silence around me, save the sweet chant of the feathered songsters in the forest, or the musical ripple of the eddying waters at my feet. I watched the majestic bluffs as they gradually faded away, through the gray twilight, from the face of day into the darker shades of night. I then turned to the rising moon as it peered above, ascending the deep blue ether, high in the heavens, casting its mellow rays over the surrounding landscape, and gilding the smooth surface of the noble river with its silvery line. I viewed with interest the stars as they appeared, one after another, in the firmament. It was then and there that I studied nature in its lonely grandeur, and saw in it the goodness of God, and felt that He who created so much beauty, and permitted the fowls of the air and the beasts of the field to roam at large and be free, never intended that man should be the slave of his fellow-man. I resolved that I would be a bondman no longer; and, taking for my guide the north star, I started for Canada, the negro's land of liberty. For many weeks I travelled by night, and lay by during the day. O, how often, while hid away in the forest, waiting for nightfall, have I thought of the beautiful lines I once heard a stranger recite: -

> 'O, hail Columbia! happy land!
> The cradle land of liberty!
> Where none but negroes bear the brand,
> Or feel the lash of slavery.
> "Then let the glorious anthem peal,
> And drown "Britannia rules the waves:"
> Strike up the song that men can feel--
> "Columbia rules four million slaves!" '

"At last I arrived at a depot of the Underground Railroad, took the express train, and here I am."

"You are welcome," said Colonel Rice, as he rose from his chair, walked to the window and looked out, as if apprehensive that the fugitive's pursuers were near by. "You are welcome," continued he; "and I will aid you on your way to Canada, for you are not safe here."

"Are you not afraid of breaking the laws by assisting this man to escape?" remarked Squire Loomis.

"I care not for laws when they stand in the way of humanity," replied the colonel.

"If you aid him in reaching Canada, and we should ever have a war with England, may be he'll take up arms and fight against his own country," said the squire.

The fugitive eyed the law-abiding man attentively for a moment, and then exclaimed, "Take up arms against my country? What country, sir, have I? The Supreme Court of the United States, and the laws of the south, doom me to be the slave of another. There is not a foot of soil over which the stars and stripes wave, where I can stand and be protected by law. I've seen my mother sold in the cattle market. I looked upon my brothers as they were driven away in chains by the slave speculator. The heavy negro whip has been applied to my own shoulders until its biting lash sunk deep into my quivering flesh. Still, sir, you call this my country. True, true, I was born in this land. My grandfather fought in the revolutionary war; my own father was in the war of 1812. Still, sir, I am a slave, a chattel, a thing, a piece of property. I've been sold in the market with horses and swine; the initials of my master's name are branded deep in this arm. Still, sir, you call this my country. And, now that I am making my escape, you feel afraid, if I reach Canada, and there should be war with England, that I will take up arms against my own country. Sir, I have no country but the grave; and I'll seek freedom there before I will again be taken back to slavery. There is no justice for me at the south; every right of my race is trampled in the dust, until humanity bleeds at every pore. I am bound for Canada, and woe to him that shall attempt to arrest me. If it comes to the worst, I will die fighting for freedom."

"I honor you for your courage," exclaimed Squire Loomis, as he sprang from his seat, and walked rapidly to and fro through the room. "It is too bad," continued he, "that such men should be enslaved in a land whose Declaration of Independence proclaims all men to be free and equal. I will aid you in any thine, that I can. What is your name?"

"I have no name," said the fugitive. "I once had a name,--it was William,--but my master's nephew came to live with him, and as I was a house servant, and the young master and I would, at times, get confused in the same name, orders were given for me to change mine. From that moment, I resolved that, as slavery had robbed me of my liberty and my name, I would not attempt to have another till I was free. So, sir, for once you have a man standing before you without a name."

## SAMUEL R. WARD.

FEW public speakers exercised greater influence in the pulpit and on the platform, in behalf of human freedom, than did Samuel R. Ward, in the early days of abolition agitation. From 1840 up to the passage of the Fugitive Slave Law, in 1850, he either preached or lectured in every church, hall, or school house in Western and Central New York. Endowed with superior mental powers, and having, through the aid of Hon. Gerrit Smith, obtained a good education, and being a close student, Mr. Ward's intellectual faculties are well developed. He was, for several years, settled over a white congregation, of the Presbyterian order, at South Butler, N. Y., where he preached with great acceptance, and was highly respected. As a speaker, he was justly held up as one of the ablest men, white or black, in the United States. The first time we ever heard him, (in 1842,) he was announced in the advertisement as "the black Daniel Webster." Standing above six feet in height, possessing a strong voice, and energetic in his gestures, Mr. Ward always impressed his highly finished and logical speeches upon his hearers. No detractor of the negro's abilities ever attributed his talents to his having Anglo-Saxon blood in his veins. As a black man, Mr. Ward was never ashamed of his complexion, but rather appeared to feel proud of it. When Captain Rynders and his followers took possession of the platform of the American Anti-Slavery Society, at their anniversary, in New York, in the spring of 1852, Frederick Douglass rose to defend the rights of the Association and the liberty of speech. Rynders objected to the speaker upon the ground that he was not a negro, but half white. Ward, being present, came forward, amid great applause, and the rowdy leader had to "knock under," and confess that genuine eloquence was not confined to the white man. William J. Wilson says of Ward, "Ideas form the basis of all Mr. Ward utters. If words and ideas are not inseparable, then, as mortar is to the stones that compose the building, so are his words to his ideas. In this, I judge, lies Mr. Ward's greatest strength. Concise without abruptness; without extraordinary stress, always clear and forcible if sparing of ornament, never inelegant,--in all, there appears a consciousness of strength, developed by close study and deep reflection, and only put forth because the occasion demands it. His appeals are directed rather to the understanding than the imagination; but so forcibly do they take possession of it, that the heart unhesitatingly yields."

Mr. Ward visited England in 1852, where he was regarded as an eloquent advocate of the rights of his race. He now resides at Kingston, Jamaica.

## SIR EDWARD JORDAN.

EDWARD JORDAN was born in Kingston, Jamaica, in the year 1798. After quitting school he entered a clothing store as a clerk; but his deep hatred to slavery, and the political and social outrages committed upon the free colored men, preyed upon his mind to such an extent that, in 1826, he associated himself with Robert Osborn, in the publication of The Watchman, a weekly newspaper devoted to the freedom and enfranchisement of the people of color. His journal was conducted with marked ability, and Mr. Jordan soon began to wield a tremendous influence against the slave power. While, absent from his editorial duties, in 1830, an article appeared in The Watchman, upon which its editor was indicted for constructive treason. He was at once arrested, placed in the dock, and arraigned for trial. He pleaded "not guilty," and asked for time to prepare for his defence. The plea was allowed, and the case was traversed to the next court. The trial came on at the appointed time; the jury was packed, for the pro-slavery element had determined on the conviction of the distinguished advocate of liberty. The whole city appeared to be lost to every thing but the proceedings of the assize. It was feared, that, if convicted, a riot would be the result, and the authorities prepared for this. A vessel of war was brought up abreast of the city, the guns of which were pointed up one of the principal streets, and at almost every avenue leading to the sea, a merchant vessel was moored, armed at least with one great gun, pointing in a similar direction,to rake the streets from bottom to top. A detachment of soldiers was kept under arms, with orders to be ready for action at a moment's warning. The officers of the court, including the judge, entered upon their duties, armed with pistols; and the sheriff was instructed to shoot the prisoner in the dock if a rescue was attempted. If convicted, Mr. Jordan's punishment was to be death. Happily for all, the verdict was "not guilty." The acquittal of the editor of The Watchman carried disappointment and dismay into the ranks of the slave oligarchy, while it gave a new impetus to the anti-slavery cause, both in Jamaica and in Great Britain, and which culminated in the abolition of slavery on the 1st of August, 1834. The following year, Mr. Jordan was elected member of the Assembly for the city of Kingston, which he still represents. About this time, The Watchman was converted into a daily paper, under the title of The Morning Journal, still in existence, and owned by Jordan and Osborn. In 1853, Mr. Jordan was elected mayor of his native city without opposition, which office he still holds. He was recently chosen premier of the island and president of the privy council.

No man is more respected in the Assembly than Mr. Jordan, and reform measures offered by him are often carried through the house, owing to the respect the members have for the introducer. In the year 1860, the honorable gentleman was elevated to the dignity of knighthood by the Queen. Sir Edward Jordan has ever been regarded as an honest, upright, and temperate man. In a literary point of view, he is considered one of the first men in Jamaica.

It is indeed a cheering sign for the negro to look at one of his race, who, a few years ago, was tried for his life in a city in which he is now the chief magistrate, inspector of the prison in which he was once incarcerated, and occupying a seat in the legislature by the side of the white man who ejected him from his position as a clerk, on account of his color. To those who say that the two races cannot live in peace together, we point to the Jamaica Assembly, with more than half of its members colored; and to all who think that the negro is only fit for servitude, we reply by saying, Look at Sir Edward Jordan.

Made in the USA
Coppell, TX
15 May 2020